Light Manufacturing in Vietnam

DIRECTIONS IN DEVELOPMENT
Private Sector Development

Light Manufacturing in Vietnam

Creating Jobs and Prosperity in a Middle-Income Economy

Hinh T. Dinh
with contributions by Deepak Mishra, Le Duy Binh, Duc Minh Pham, and
Pham Thi Thu Hang

THE WORLD BANK
Washington, D.C.

Contents

Box

Figures

Tables

Foreword

Vietnam is at a crossroads. While the economic reforms of the last 25 years have helped achieve a substantial reduction in poverty and raised the country from low-income to lower-middle-income status, the impetus of the reforms is no longer sufficient to maintain rapid economic growth and create jobs. The current growth model is grounded in the state-owned sector and in an emphasis on quantity rather than quality to drive economic progress based on low-cost labor and the assembly of products for export. Economic growth has been slowing since the global financial crisis of 2008–09, and macroeconomic vulnerabilities are evident. The old model has run its course.

Light Manufacturing in Vietnam argues that to return the economy to a path of rapid economic growth and to create quality jobs will require a structural transformation that can lift workers from low-productivity agriculture and the mere assembly of imported inputs to higher-productivity activities. The country needs to address fundamental issues in the manufacturing sector that have been masked by past economic growth. Addressing these issues would help Vietnam move up the higher–value added chain and avoid the middle-income trap experienced by some other middle-income economies, including in East Asia. Boosting productivity by enhancing the quality of the labor force, changing the structure of industry through a reduction in the influence of state-owned enterprises, promoting foreign direct investment in upstream activities, and helping domestic private enterprises integrate with the national and global economy through the establishment of industrial parks, industrial clusters, and trading companies are a step forward in this effort.

Based on a wide array of quantitative and qualitative techniques, *Light Manufacturing in Vietnam* identifies key constraints on manufacturing growth in Vietnam and evaluates differences in firm performance between China and Vietnam. The book shows that there is a dichotomy between domestic enterprises and the enterprises supported by foreign direct investment. The dominant state-owned enterprises and foreign-invested firms are often not integrated with smaller domestic firms through backward or forward links in the use of domestically produced inputs or intermediate products. Growth in the domestic light manufacturing sector has arisen from the sheer number of micro and small enterprises rather than from expansion in the number of medium and large firms. Final products have little value added; technology and expertise are not shared; and the economy has failed to move up the structural transformation ladder. This structure of production is one of the reasons Vietnam's rapid process of industrialization over the last three decades has not been accompanied by a favorable trade balance.

Policy measures to solve problems in competitiveness in Vietnam must address the structure of the light manufacturing sector discussed above, while raising the value added of the industry. To that end, steps must be taken to nurture the expansion of small domestic firms while helping these firms to achieve greater productivity through trade integration. This will require improvements in labor skills and technology and in the quality and variety of products able to compete with imports. Policies to reduce the role of the state-owned sector, promote trading companies, encourage clustering and subcontracting, and expand foreign and social networking are important in this respect. To raise the value added of its goods, Vietnam needs to integrate the supply chain of assembly activities by investing in the upstream production of the goods—such as processed agriculture, garments, and wood—in which it has a comparative advantage and for which it has already established a market share. Unlike downstream activities, however, the production of the associated raw materials and intermediate goods is capital intensive and technology driven and calls for skilled labor. Inviting foreign direct investment into these areas and reforming education and vocational systems are the best means to reach this goal. For this reason, a complete review of the incentives for foreign direct investment is needed to focus on upstream production and on bringing in capital and technical expertise, while improving labor and entrepreneurial skills.

The book relies on detailed value chain analyses that were carried out in five industries at the core of the Vietnamese light manufacturing sector: agribusiness, leather, wood processing and wood products, metal products, and apparel. Based on these analyses, *Light Manufacturing in Vietnam* proposes concrete policy measures to help policy makers identify, prioritize, and resolve the most serious constraints in these specific light manufacturing industries.

Light Manufacturing in Vietnam has several innovative features. First, it provides in-depth cost comparisons between China and Vietnam at the sectoral and product levels. Second, the book uses a wide array of quantitative and qualitative techniques, as well as a focused approach, to identify specific key constraints in the most promising light manufacturing sectors and to evaluate differences in the performance of firms in the two countries. Third, it proposes market-based measures and selective government intervention to ease these constraints. Fourth, it highlights the interconnectedness of constraints and solutions. For example, solving the manufacturing input problem requires actions in agriculture, education, and infrastructure. It is hoped that this book will encourage policy makers, entrepreneurs, and workers in Vietnam to think creatively to capture the opportunities of the manufacturing sector and accelerate economic growth.

Victoria Kwakwa
Country Director for Vietnam
The World Bank

Acknowledgments

This book has been prepared by a team composed of Hinh T. Dinh (Team Leader), Deepak K. Mishra, Le Duy Binh, Duc Minh Pham, and Pham Thi Thu Hang. Key inputs for the comparative value chain analysis have been provided by Global Development Solutions, LLC of Reston, Virginia, under the direction of Yasuo Konishi and Glen Surabian. Quang Hong Doan, Kathleen Fitzgerald, Ephraim Kebede, Eleonora Mavroeidi, Chi Do Pham, Thach Ngoc Pham, and Van Can Thai have contributed greatly to the work. The book is part of a larger World Bank project on Light Manufacturing in Africa conducted by a core team consisting of Hinh T. Dinh (Team Leader), Vincent Palmade (Co-Team Leader), Vandana Chandra, Frances Cossar, Tugba Gurcanlar, Ali Zafar, Eleonora Mavroeidi, Kathleen Fitzgerald, and Gabriela Calderon Motta. The report has benefited from valuable comments by Victoria Kwakwa (Country Director for Vietnam); Sameer Goyal (Senior Financial Sector Specialist); Habib Nasser Rab (Senior Economist); Pham Van Thuyet (World Bank retiree); and participants at the Workshop on Trade Facilitation, Value Creation, and Competitiveness held in Hanoi in December 2012. In particular, we would like to thank Tran Minh Thu (Senior Official, Light Industry Department, Ministry of Industry and Trade) and Dang Kim Dung (General Secretary, Vietnam Garment and Textile Association) for their valuable comments. The work has been carried out with the support and guidance of the following senior managers of the World Bank: Kaushik Basu (Senior Vice President and Chief Economist), Justin Yifu Lin (former Senior Vice President and Chief Economist), Axel van Trotsenburg (Vice President, East Asia and Pacific Region), Victoria Kwakwa (Country Director for Vietnam), Sudhir Shetty (Director, Poverty Reduction and Economic Management), Zia Qureshi (Director, Operations and Strategy Department, Development Economics), Gaiv Tata (Director, Africa Finance and Private Sector Development), Marilou Uy (Senior Advisor, Special Envoy Office and former Director, Africa Finance and Private Sector Development), and Tunc Tahsin Uyanik (Director, East Asia and Pacific Finance and Private Sector Development). We thank the following colleagues for their unfailing encouragement and support: Han T. Dinh, Alphonsus J. Marcelis, Célestin Monga, Ha Minh Nguyen, Martin Rama, David Rosenblatt, Geremie Sawadogo, Tran Kim Chi, Dipankar Megh Bhanot, Aban Daruwala, Saida Doumbia Gall, Nancy Lim, Le Thi Khanh Linh, and Melanie Brah Marie Melindji.

The team would like to thank the many people who have advised, guided, and supported the work throughout the preparation of this book. In particular, we are grateful to those people who generously gave their time to discuss and to be interviewed by us. We owe special thanks to the following staff members from the Vietnamese Chamber of Commerce and Industry who arranged the interviews: Doan Thuy Nga, Doan Thi Quyen, Dang Thanh Tung, and Pham Dinh Vu.

The report has been edited by a team headed by Bruce Ross-Larson, Meta de Coquereaumont, and Robert Zimmermann. The team thanks Paola Scalabrin and Kristen Iovino for excellent production support of the book. The financial support of the World Bank–Netherlands Partnership Program and the Japan Policy and Human Resources Development Fund is gratefully acknowledged.

About the Author

Hinh T. Dinh is Lead Economist in the Office of the Senior Vice President and Chief Economist of the World Bank. Previously, he served as Lead Economist in the Africa Region (1998–2008), the Finance Complex (1991–98), and the Middle East Region at the Bank (1979–91). He received his undergraduate degrees with high honors in economics and mathematics from the State University of New York and his MA in economics, MS in industrial engineering, and PhD in Economics from the University of Pittsburgh (1978). His research focuses on public finance, international finance, industrialization, and economic development. His latest books include *Light Manufacturing in Africa* (2012), *Performance of Manufacturing Firms in Africa* (2012), *Light Manufacturing in Zambia* (2013), *Light Manufacturing in Tanzania* (2013), and *Tales from the Development Frontier* (2013).

About the Contributors

Deepak Mishra is Lead Economist in the World Bank's Washington, DC headquarters, where he oversees economic policy work for the East Asia and Pacific Region. He was the Bank's Lead Economist for Vietnam, based in Hanoi, between 2010 and 2013. He holds an MA in economics from the Delhi School of Economics and a PhD in Economics from the University of Maryland. Before joining the Bank, Deepak worked at the Federal Reserve Board, Tata Motors, and the University of Maryland.

Le Duy Binh is an Economist at Economica Vietnam, a private consulting and research firm specializing in development economics. In 2000–09, he worked for the Deutsche Gesellschaft für Internationale Zusammenarbeit as Senior Advisor on enterprise and private sector development. Before that, he worked for the Japan Bank for International Cooperation, the National Economics University, and the State Bank of Vietnam. His research covers enterprise development, the private sector, finance, development banking, and governance.

Duc Minh Pham has 18 years of experience working in the World Bank on Vietnam and other East Asia and Pacific countries, including Cambodia, Myanmar, and the Philippines. He leads analytical work; coordinates policy dialogue with client governments; and prepares reports on strategic planning, structural adjustment, trade liberalization and competitiveness, and revenue management. His recent focus has been on trade development and tax policy and administration. He holds a master's degree in business administration from the University of Illinois at Champaign-Urbana.

Pham Thi Thu Hang is Secretary General of the Vietnam Chamber of Commerce and Industry (VCCI). Previously, she was Director of the Small and Medium Enterprises Promotion Center and Director of the Enterprise Development Foundation of VCCI. She has managed projects in small and medium enterprise development, support for industries, the supplier chain, and women entrepreneurship for VCCI, in collaboration with the Asian Development Bank, the United Nations Development Programme, the U.S.

Agency for International Development, the World Bank Group, and many other organizations. She holds a PhD in Economics (1990) from Moscow State University and is a member of the Association of Southeast Asian Nations SME Advisory Board. She was Editor-in-Chief of the *Vietnam Annual Business Report* between 2006 and 2012.

Abbreviations

CMT	cut, make, and trim
FDI	foreign direct investment
FOB	free on board
GDP	gross domestic product
GDVT	General Department of Vocational Training (Vietnam)
MOET	Ministry of Education and Training (Vietnam)
MOLISA	Ministry of Labor, Invalids, and Social Affairs (Vietnam)
SAR	special administrative region (China)
SME	small and medium enterprise
SOE	state-owned enterprise
TPP	Trans-Pacific Partnership
TVET	technical vocational education and training
Vinatex	Vietnam National Textile and Garment Group

All dollar amounts are U.S. dollars ($) unless otherwise indicated. Where other currencies are used, the conversion to U.S. dollars relies on the average exchange rate for the year concerned (line rh in International Financial Statistics [database], International Monetary Fund, Washington, DC, http://elibrary-data.imf .org/FindDataReports.aspx?d=33061&e=169393).

Note on Vietnamese names: In Vietnam and many other Asian countries, the family name is typically written before the given name in most everyday contexts. We have adopted this practice here for our Vietnamese interviewees and authors who are living or active mainly in Vietnam and who are not otherwise known by a Westernized name. These individuals are shown in the reference lists without the standard comma between the family name and the first name (thus, Le Duy Binh, family name first; no comma). Individuals who have followed the Westernized name order and who are known in this way are presented as such in the text (thus, Hinh T. Dinh with Dinh as family name). Their names are shown in reference lists with the standard comma included (thus, Dinh, Hinh T.).

Overview

This book aims to answer the following questions:

- What are the binding constraints facing light manufacturing in Vietnam?
- How have firms coped with these constraints?
- Which practical policy reforms would help firms overcome the constraints and jump-start industry to facilitate the transformation of Vietnam into a modern economy?

The book explores these issues at the country, sectoral, and product levels.

Industry and Country Focus

The book focuses on five light manufacturing industries that form the core of the Vietnamese industrial sector: processed foods and beverages (agribusiness), leather, wood processing and wood products, metal products, and apparel.

Because it is the world's most competitive country in light manufacturing and a fierce competitor in many domestic markets throughout the world, we have chosen China as the benchmark for an in-depth study of the cost structure of production in Vietnam. China is a relevant comparator because, when it emerged in global markets, it had to adapt to compete in manufactured goods that were dominated by others (Hong Kong SAR, China; the Republic of Korea; Singapore; and Taiwan, China). China successfully moved from cheap, labor-intensive goods to higher–value added goods. It also shared many of the investment climate constraints currently prevailing in Vietnam.

Methodology

The study draws on five analytical tools applied in 2010–11 and presented online:

- New research based on the World Bank Enterprise Surveys.[1]
- Qualitative interviews conducted by the study team at around 130 formal and informal enterprises of all sizes in China and Vietnam. The interviews were

based on a questionnaire designed by John Sutton of the London School of Economics.

- Quantitative interviews conducted by the Vietnamese Chamber of Commerce and Industry for Oxford University at around 600 formal and informal enterprises of all sizes in China and Vietnam. The interviews were based on a questionnaire designed by Marcel Fafchamps and Simon Quinn (2012) of Oxford University.
- In-depth interviews at about 140 formal medium enterprises by Global Development Solutions, a consulting firm, for a detailed comparative value chain analysis (GDS 2011). Data were collected in China and Vietnam between July 2010 and February 2011.
- A Kaizen study on the impact of managerial training among owners of small and medium enterprises (SMEs) (World Bank 2011). The training, delivered to about 250 entrepreneurs in Vietnam, was led by Japanese researchers at the Foundation for Advanced Studies on International Development and the National Graduate Institute for Policy Studies, both located in Tokyo.

The analysis in chapters 4–8 is supported by these five data sources, while the analysis in chapters 1–3 relies on country and international data.

Note

1. See Enterprise Surveys (database), International Finance Corporation and World Bank, Washington, DC, http://www.enterprisesurveys.org.

References

Fafchamps, Marcel, and Simon Quinn. 2012. "Results of Sample Surveys of Firms." In *Performance of Manufacturing Firms in Africa: An Empirical Analysis*, edited by Hinh T. Dinh and George R. G. Clarke, 139–211. Washington, DC: World Bank.

GDS (Global Development Solutions). 2011. *The Value Chain and Feasibility Analysis; Domestic Resource Cost Analysis*. Vol. 2 of *Light Manufacturing in Africa: Targeted Policies to Enhance Private Investment and Create Jobs*. Washington, DC: World Bank. http://go.worldbank.org/6G2A3TFI20.

World Bank. 2011. *Kaizen for Managerial Skills Improvement in Small and Medium Enterprises: An Impact Evaluation Study*. Vol. 4 of *Light Manufacturing in Africa: Targeted Policies to Enhance Private Investment and Create Jobs*. Washington, DC: World Bank. http://go.worldbank.org/4Y1QF5FIB0.

CHAPTER 1

Industrial Growth in the Overall Development Context

This chapter surveys Vietnam's economic development path over the last 25 years and examines the country's major challenges in the coming decade. It reviews the progress and the setbacks since the *Doi Moi* policy reforms were implemented in 1986, including macroeconomic problems that emerged in 2008.[1] It analyzes the roots of the recent policy challenges and traces them to the weak microeconomic foundation of industry, the focus of this book.

Growth and Structural Transformation

In less than 25 years, economic reforms have altered Vietnam from one of the world's lowest income countries to a lower-middle-income country. In 2011, the country's per capita income reached $1,407, up from $437 in 1986, while gross domestic product (GDP) grew an average of 7 percent a year during the period (World Bank 2012). This rapid expansion followed the Doi Moi reforms of 1986, which changed the centrally planned economy into a market-oriented economy more well integrated in the world economy. Land use rights were granted; customs tariffs were instituted; and the establishment of private enterprises was supported, along with the removal of most quotas. Subsequent reforms have sought to open trade even more, including by reducing tariff and nontariff barriers on imports and exports, which has allowed strong export growth. With its accession to the World Trade Organization in 2007, Vietnam became a source and destination of large trade flows and a recipient of substantial foreign direct investment (FDI), which was equivalent to 20 percent of GDP in 2011. Net FDI commitments to Vietnam have, since the World Trade Organization accession, exceeded those to Indonesia, the Philippines, and Thailand combined (World Bank 2012). Poverty fell rapidly, from 58 percent of the population in 1993 to only 11 percent in 2010 (UNIDO and MPI 2012).

However, since 2008, Vietnam has faced major challenges in restoring macroeconomic balances and sustaining high economic growth. Over 2008–11, the country's economic growth declined to an average of 6.1 percent a year from

8.1 percent a year during the previous five years. Global integration has led to greater economic volatility, and Vietnam has become more susceptible to output fluctuations among its trading partners at a time when the latter are experiencing significant recession. Vietnamese authorities have responded by adopting a stimulus package, which has temporarily supported growth, but done little to restore long-term macrostability.

A detailed analysis shows that the economy underwent some structural transformation over 2000–11, though this was not significant (table 1.1). The structure of national output in 2011 reflected an economy that was transitioning out of agriculture. In current prices, the share of industry, broadly defined to include mining, manufacturing, electricity, and construction, rose only slightly during the period, from 37.8 percent to 40.5 percent of GDP, while the share of manufacturing in GDP barely increased. The analysis in nominal shares may mask the true extent of structural transformation because manufacturing prices tend to grow more slowly than the prices of services. Indeed, if such an analysis is carried out in constant terms, the share of manufacturing rose from 20 percent to 25 percent over the period.

Compared with China and other Asian countries, Vietnam's export basket failed to expand into medium- and high-technology products over 1980–2009, though some low-technology products emerged (figure 1.1).

A look at Vietnam's exports reveals that the technological intensity of the majority is low (figure 1.2, panel a). The share of high-technology goods is increasing, but at a slow rate; the majority of exports use no technology at all. China, meanwhile, has successfully transitioned most of its export production into technology-intensive goods (figure 1.2, panel b).

Figure 1.2 also illustrates the role of low-technology production in developing economies. While China has undertaken greater production of high-technology goods than Vietnam, low-technology goods still make up a sizable proportion of China's exports. However, as more high-technology goods are introduced, low-technology goods lose importance. Low-technology production is thus an important stepping-stone to higher-intensity manufacturing.[2]

Some progress has been made recently in Vietnam. According to Customs Office statistics, Vietnam's exports of high-technology commodities such as

Table 1.1 Sectoral Composition of GDP Growth, Vietnam, 2000–11
Percent

Sector	Growth rate 2000–11	Share of GDP		
		2000–02	2008–11	2008–11, constant prices
Agriculture	3.6	23.6	21.4	17.7
Industry	8.9	37.8	40.5	43.4
Manufacturing	10.2	19.6	19.8	25.0
Services	7.2	38.6	38.1	38.8
Total	7.1	100.0	100.0	100.0

Source: World Bank 2012.
Note: Values are in current prices except where noted. GDP = gross domestic product.

Figure 1.1 Top Five Exports, Selected Asian Economies, 1980–85 and 2005–09

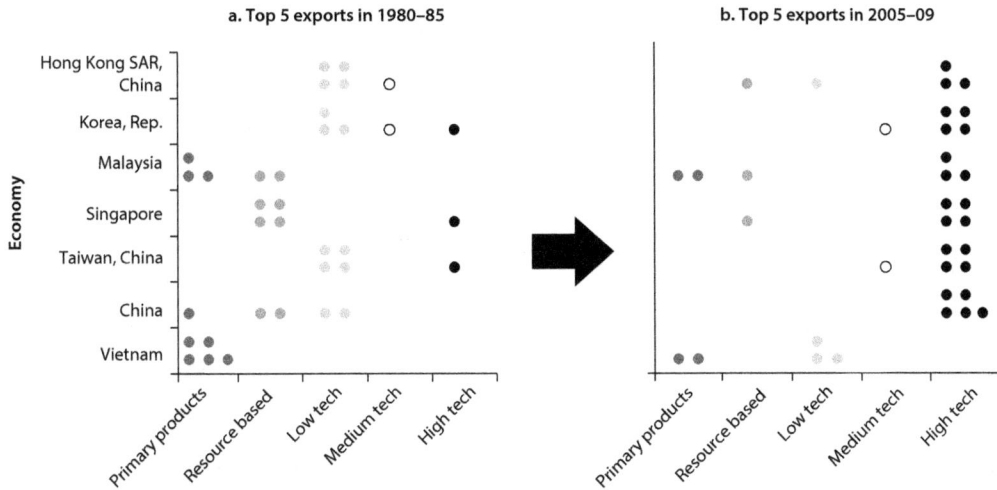

a. Top 5 exports in 1980–85

b. Top 5 exports in 2005–09

Source: Economic Diversification and Growth in Developing Countries: Toolkit (webtool), World Bank, Washington, DC, http://info.worldbank .org/etools/prmed.

Figure 1.2 Share of Technological Intensity in Total Exports, China and Vietnam, 2000–11

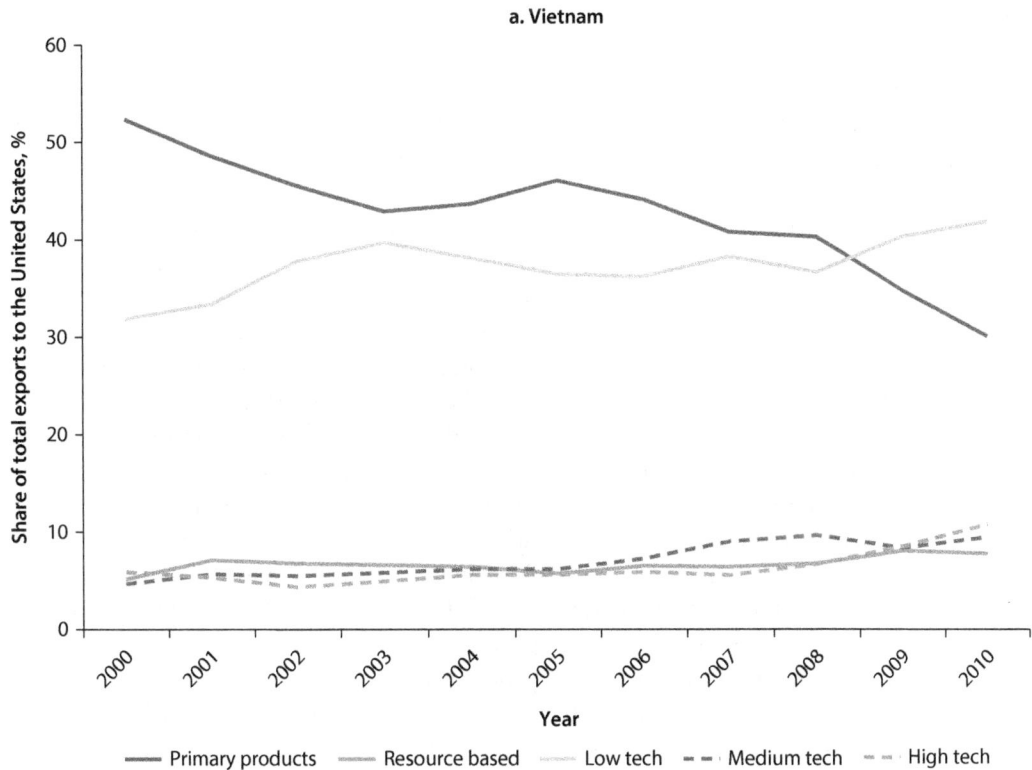

a. Vietnam

Figure continues next page

Figure 1.2 Share of Technological Intensity in Total Exports, China and Vietnam, 2000–11 (continued)

b. China

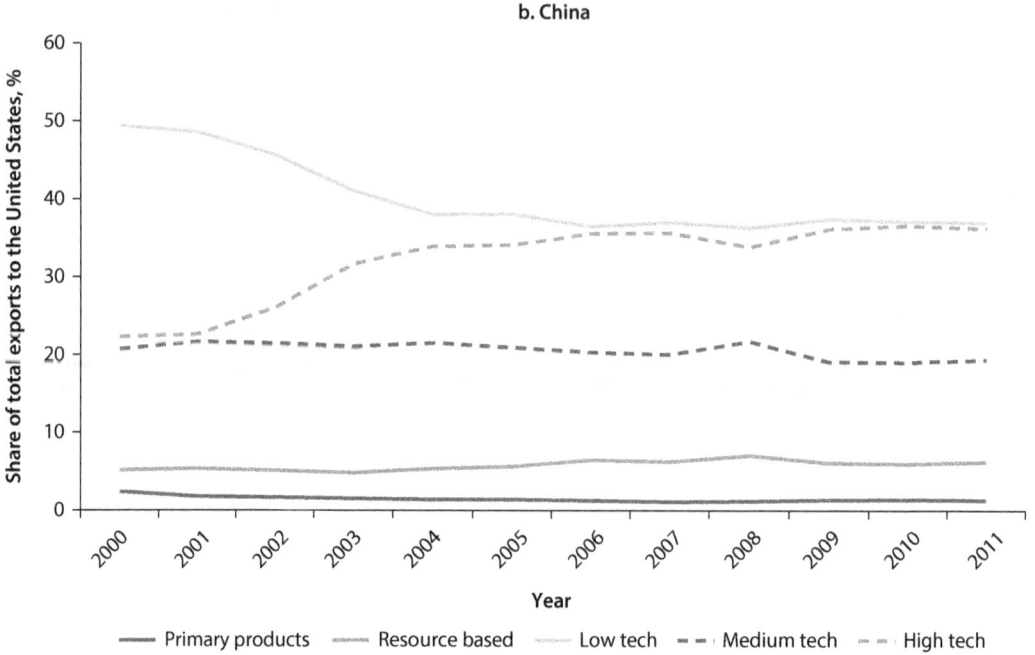

Source: Based on data of WITS (World Integrated Trade Solutions) (database), World Bank, Washington, DC, http://wits.worldbank.org/WITS.

computers, electrical products, telephones, mobile phones, and video cameras reached $22.2 billion in 2012, almost twice the 2011 level of $11.7 billion. Of this amount, phones and their components accounted for more than $12.7 billion, almost twice the previous year's level, and exports of computers, electronic products, and the associated components reached more than $7 billion, up almost 70 percent. The next largest high-technology export group includes cameras, camcorders, and the associated components and represented about $1.7 billion, up more than 140 percent.

Yet, there is a huge difference between exports of high-technology products and gains in terms of the value added created during this process. In Vietnam, high-technology products are produced mainly by foreign-invested firms, such as Intel and Samsung, that use Vietnamese labor to carry out assembly-type work, sometimes through subcontracts. For example, Samsung's mobile phone facility in Bac Ninh, which produces all the company's latest high-technology products such as the Galaxy S III, the Galaxy Tab 7, and the Galaxy Tab 10, accounted for exports worth almost $10 billion in 2012, but obtains almost all the accessories and parts from abroad.

To illustrate this feature of production, figure 1.3 shows the value added accounted for by China in the exportation of a $500 made-in-China iPhone. China reaps a proportionately small share of the profit from this manufacturing process. The Chinese workers in this case perform production tasks that are similar to those carried out by Vietnamese workers in Samsung's scheme.

Figure 1.3 The Production Value Chain of an iPhone Made in China

Retail price, $500, of which the manufacturing
cost is $178.96 broken down by country

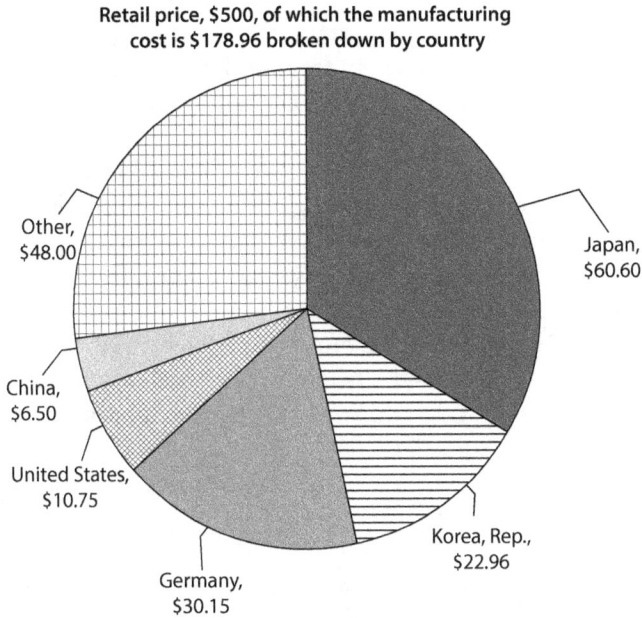

- Other, $48.00
- Japan, $60.60
- China, $6.50
- United States, $10.75
- Korea, Rep., $22.96
- Germany, $30.15

Source: Data from Rassweiler 2009.

Hence, although the recent progress is noteworthy, Vietnam should mature beyond final assembly production to gain more value added in output. Vietnamese enterprises should thus increase investment in the manufacturing of spare parts, components, and accessories in the production of phones, for example. However, this will require associated capital-intensive investments and higher-level skills. So, it is important to encourage FDI in these areas, while intensifying reforms in education and training.

This deepening structural transformation will allow Vietnam to achieve the goals in industrialization laid out in the Socio-Economic Development Strategy for the Period of 2011–20 (Vietnam 2011, 9), which calls for rapid industrialization by assigning "priority to the development of products [that] have competitive advantage and [the] possibility to join in the production network and global value chain in such industries as high technology, mechanics, information and communications technology, and pharmaceuticals." It will also help Vietnam avoid becoming a long-term, low-wage producer.

The Economic Impact of the Global Financial Crisis

Vietnam's economic growth has slowed since the 2008–09 global financial crisis. In 2008, the country's GDP growth rate dropped to 6 percent. This was associated especially with a downturn in the property market that more than offset a rise in agricultural production. Industrial production also contracted, particularly in the foreign-invested sector. Inflation, which had hovered around 8 percent a year, peaked at 20 percent in 2008 because of commodity price increases in the first part of the year, as well as other destabilizing factors, notably the impact of large capital inflows in 2007, which led to excessive domestic spending. The current account deficit rose in 2008 because of high global commodity prices; this was financed by significant capital inflows, especially FDI.

However, our analysis shows that the economic slowdown and the problems in macrostability did not originate in the global crisis. Instead, they were associated with more fundamental structural issues that were masked by the economic growth of previous years. These issues persist, and, unless they are resolved fully, it will be impossible to continue on the high-growth path of the past. Addressing these issues would also help Vietnam move up the higher–value added chain and avoid the middle income trap—the failure to graduate into the group of industrialized countries—with which other East Asian economies, such as Malaysia and Thailand, have been struggling.

Until now, Vietnam has pursued economic growth through two main strategies:

- Reliance on a high ratio of investment to GDP, while focusing on the volume rather than on the depth of investment through high-quality, high-return projects.
- Most investments are sourced through the public sector, including capital outlays financed through the budget and by state-owned enterprises (SOEs), which have been provided with easy access to bank credit at privileged interest rates. In contrast, the private sector, while contributing about 50 percent to GDP and absorbing almost 90 percent of the active labor force, has received only limited access to credit and must succeed on an uneven playing field with respect to public enterprises (Nguyen 2012). This biased pattern of investment and production imposes severe limitations on the economy's efficiency and is the cause of serious distortions in overall credit allocation.

The Inherent Low Efficiency of the Economy

The development strategy of the recent past has thus been led by heavy public investment. SOEs have played the major role, and private initiatives have been lacking as an engine of growth. The reason behind the lack of a micro-foundation in industrial development is the relative absence of rational private sector decisions and of a private sector market orientation. Economic growth has depended on capital investment rather than productivity, in marked contrast with China. In the 1990s, total factor productivity accounted for 44 percent of the country's GDP growth, but the share declined to 26 percent in the first decade of the 2000s (see chapter 2). During the same period, the contribution of capital increased from 34 percent to 53 percent. Meanwhile, the contribution of total factor productivity to economic growth in China was over 50 percent.

Moreover, in Vietnam, the dominant SOEs and FDI firms—the key players—are often not integrated with smaller firms through backward or forward links in domestically produced inputs or intermediate products. Consequently, final products have little value added; technology and expertise are not shared; and the economy fails to move up the structural transformation ladder. In contrast, much of the success of recently transforming economies, such as China, has revolved around the strong production links between smaller and larger firms in the private sector.

While other Asian countries have rebounded from the global recession, Vietnam struggled with GDP growth of 6.8 percent in 2010 and 5.9 percent in 2011, well below the 7 percent average of the previous decade. By Asian standards, macroeconomic instability worsened despite a high ratio of investment to GDP, which reached almost 39.0 percent in 2010 and only fell to 34.6 percent in 2011 because the government began to take a more serious view of public spending. Although capital continued to be a major contributor to growth, its contribution was declining (Nguyen 2012). This point is further illustrated by the steady increase in the incremental capital-output ratio, which measures the efficiency of investment relative to output. This ratio rose from 4.9 over 2000–05 to 7.4 over 2006–10 (Bui 2012).

The Production Pattern, Trade Deficit, and Low Value Addition

The overall pattern of production has also depended heavily on imports of raw materials and intermediate inputs, and this has caused persistent annual trade deficits despite two decades of steady economic growth, unlike China and most neighboring countries, where trade surpluses have followed after years of development. In Vietnam, notably, the output of the highly favored FDI companies—which represent a significant share of total investment capital and exports—typically has a substantial import content because these companies tend to use imports to meet their material needs and only rely on the advantage of low-wage local labor to produce exports. This is another important feature in the current production pattern that has contributed to low value added and trade imbalances.

Unlike other developing countries, Vietnam has consistently experienced large and widening trade deficits. Normally, in the early stages of economic development, a country must import large quantities of the machinery and equipment needed for growth. Then, as the economy develops, the trade deficit narrows to zero or becomes a surplus. Over 1990–2010, only Vietnam and Thailand had trade deficits for more than two or three years, and, since 1998, Thailand has achieved a trade surplus (figure 1.4). However, in Vietnam, the high-deficit pattern has continued unabated since the country embarked on Doi Moi in 1986. Worse, the deficits have shown a tendency to widen over the last decade.

There are three reasons for the persistence of the country's trade deficit. The first is the dependence of exports on imported raw materials and imported

Figure 1.4 Trade Balances, Selected Asian Countries, 1990–2010

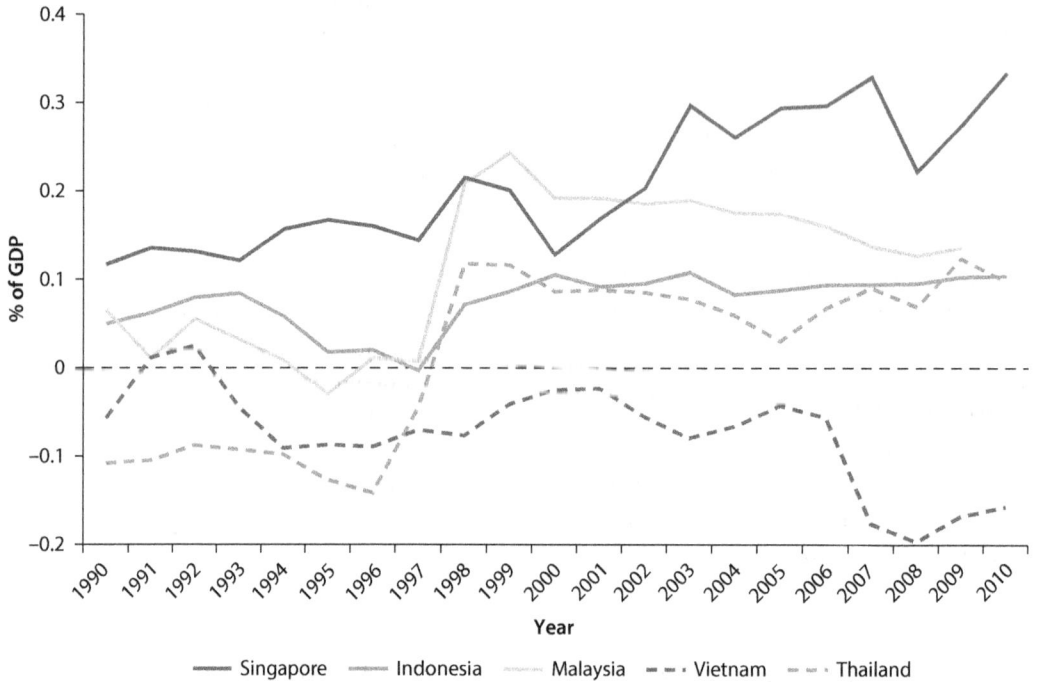

Source: World Bank 2012.
Note: GDP = gross domestic product.

intermediate products. Export activities rely almost exclusively on imported inputs, and, generally, the only local contribution is low-skilled workers (Ketels and others 2010). The exceptions are exports of natural resources and agricultural products. Figure 1.5 compares the patterns in the trade balance and net exports to GDP and shows they are the same. In the apparel sector, imported inputs are used in the manufacture of 70–80 percent of all exports.

Second, Vietnam has not been able to advance beyond the low–value added development model whereby it provides a large pool of cheap labor, which, in combination with capital and technology from abroad, turns out cheap products for export. Without a shift toward a growth model based on productivity and competitiveness, Vietnamese labor will be condemned to low wages because, should real wages rise, production could easily be transplanted to countries where cheap labor is still readily available, such as Bangladesh or Cambodia.

Third, most exports are produced by enterprises that are supported by foreign investment and that have little or no connection to the vast majority of local enterprises, which are characterized by low productivity and produce low-quality products for the domestic market. The benefits of foreign technology and foreign expertise have therefore not permeated into the domestic sector, which happens to be the country's largest employer (chapter 2).

Figure 1.5 Trade Balance and Net Exports to GDP, Vietnam, 1996–2011

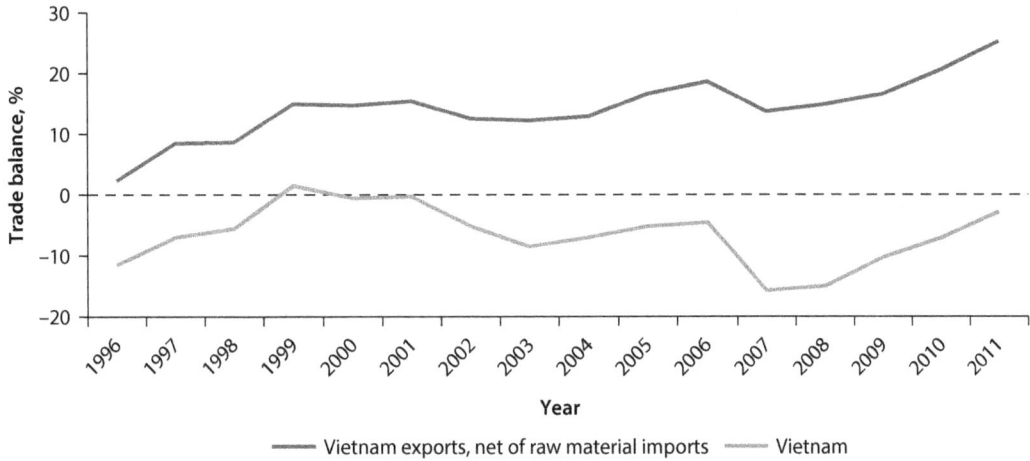

Sources: Monthly Statistical Information (database), General Statistical Office of Vietnam, Hanoi, http://www.gso.gov.vn/default_en
.aspx?tabid=622; World Bank 2012.
Note: Exports, net of raw material imports, underestimate net exports because they do not take into account the imports of intermediate goods.
GDP = gross domestic product.

The bias against local companies becomes more pronounced if the devaluation of the exchange rate is taken into account. Unlike the foreign-invested companies, the input costs of local companies have risen because of the devaluation, and this has not been offset by any tariff reduction or output price increases. Moreover, any output price adjustments undertaken by local companies to compensate are subject to government control.

Exchange rates are an important determinant of international competitiveness; relative changes in real effective exchange rates contribute to changes in the relative competitiveness of export sectors across countries. Figure 1.6 shows trends in the real effective exchange rates of the Chinese yuan and the Vietnamese dong over the last decade. Relative to the yuan, the dong still shows appreciation in the effective exchange rate, therefore making it difficult for non-FDI domestic producers to compete.

The large and widening trade deficit, along with dwindling reserves, has put pressure on the exchange rate in recent years and makes the task of macroeconomic management difficult. The authorities must walk a fine line between keeping a stable exchange rate to hold down inflation and maintaining a competitive exchange rate for exports. They need to avoid the experience of the East Asian countries during the 1997–98 crisis, when some governments insisted on using administrative controls to peg the exchange rate, causing speculative tendencies to emerge; under weak macroeconomic management, a situation could then easily develop whereby any devaluation would be viewed as insufficient (too little, too late), causing a loss in confidence that would be aggravated by the weak banking sector and lead to a free fall.

Figure 1.6 Changes in the Real Effective Exchange Rate, Chinese Yuan and Vietnamese Dong, 2000–10

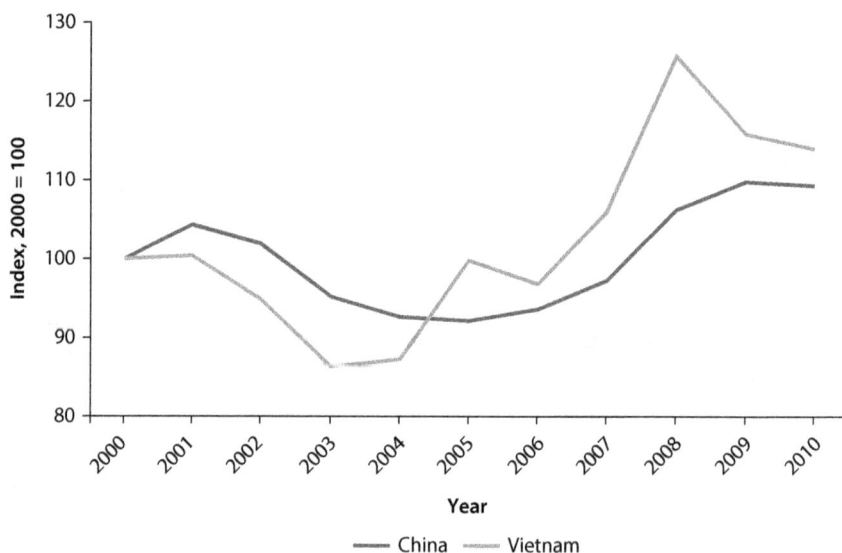

Source: International Financial Statistics (database), International Monetary Fund, Washington, DC, http://elibrary-data
.imf.org/FindDataReports.aspx?d=33061&e=169393.
Note: An increase signifies appreciation.

As Vietnam has become more open, economic policy coordination has become more complicated and requires skillful management. In particular, Vietnam has to confront three problems simultaneously: pressures on the exchange rate to depreciate because of the trade deficit, pressures on the exchange rate (in the opposite direction) because of capital inflows, and pressures on domestic economic policies (mainly monetary policy) for economic growth (and employment creation).

Notes

1. The Doi Moi (renovation) reforms were aimed at transitioning the planned economy to a market-oriented economy.

2. Note that this is not the same as the transition from lower– to higher–value added goods because a country can still have low value added in the production of high-technology goods—such as the assembly work in China on Apple iPads and iPhones—or high value added in the production of low-technology goods.

References

Bui, Trinh. 2012. "Re-Evaluation of Investment Efficiency in Public and Private Sectors and Policy Implications." In *Economic Stabilization and Growth: Analysis of Macroeconomic Policies*, edited by Pham Do Chi and Dao Van Hung. Hanoi:

Development and Policies Research Center and Science and Technology Publishing House.

Ketels, Christian, Nguyen Dinh Cung, Nguyen Thi Tue Anh, and Do Hong Hanh. 2010. *Vietnam Competitiveness Report 2010*. Singapore: Asia Competitiveness Institute, Lee Kuan Yew School of Public Policy, National University of Singapore. http://www.isc .hbs.edu/pdf/Vietnam_Competitiveness_Report_2010_Eng.pdf.

Nguyen, Phuong Thao. 2012. "Growth Based on Capital Investment: Is It Done the Right Way?" *Economy and Forecast Review* 12, Ministry of Planning and Investment, Hanoi.

Rassweiler, Andrew. 2009. "iPhone 3G S Carries $178.96 BOM and Manufacturing Cost, iSuppli Teardown Reveals." Press release, June 4, IHS iSuppli, Englewood, CO. http://www.isuppli.com/Teardowns/News/Pages/iPhone-3G-S-Carries-178-96 -BOM-and-Manufacturing-Cost-iSuppli-Teardown-Reveals.aspx.

UNIDO (United Nations Industrial Development Organization) and MPI (Vietnam, Ministry of Planning and Investment). 2012. *Viet Nam Industrial Investment Report 2011: Understanding the Impact of Foreign Direct Investment on Industrial Development*. Vienna: UNIDO. http://www.unido.org/fileadmin/user_media/Publications/Pub _free/VIIR%20print.pdf.

Vietnam, 11th National Congress of the Communist Party of Vietnam. 2011. "Vietnam's Socio-Economic Development Strategy for the Period of 2011–2020." Hanoi. http:// www.economica.vn/Portals/0/MauBieu/1d3f7ee0400e42152bdcaa439bf62686.pdf.

World Bank. 2012. *World Development Indicators 2012*. April. Washington, DC: World Bank. http://data.worldbank.org/sites/default/files/wdi-2012-ebook.pdf.

CHAPTER 2

Industrial Structure and Sectoral Issues

This volume focuses on light manufacturing in Vietnam because labor-intensive light manufacturing can absorb the more than a million young entrants into the labor force each year and also because light manufacturing represents a springboard for higher–value added, technologically advanced industries. While light manufacturing is not the only alternative to low-productivity agriculture, it is an important source of growth and productive employment in economies with a comparative advantage in labor-intensive sectors.[1] In almost every country, the transition from traditional agriculture to a modern economy began with light manufacturing: cotton and silk textiles in Japan; textiles, food processing, and a host of labor-intensive consumer products in Taiwan, China; and so on. This is because of light manufacturing's potential to absorb quickly a large pool of less-skilled workers from agriculture into new occupations that substantially increase worker productivity without imposing steep capital requirements.

Thus, similar to the situation during the 1960s, when the rising costs of land and labor diminished the comparative advantage of light industry in Japan and opened the door to the rapid expansion of the production of labor-intensive export goods in Hong Kong SAR, China; the Republic of Korea; Singapore; and Taiwan, China, the rapid cost escalation now facing these same economies is creating an opportunity for Vietnam to undertake a profound structural transformation. The challenge facing Vietnam from this perspective is to identify how best to transform the economy so that it no longer relies on inexpensive, low-skilled labor, but on a more productive, higher–value added, modern industrial base.

The next section discusses the manufacturing context and compares one of the world's most competitive producers, China, with Vietnam. It illustrates some successes in China and compares them with selected cases in Vietnam. The subsequent section focuses on the characteristics of light manufacturing in Vietnam, particularly in relation to the case of China, and describes the constraints in five major sectors.

The International Context of Manufacturing: China and Vietnam

The prospects of light manufacturing in Vietnam must be viewed in the context of the global growth of light manufacturing over the past two decades and the conditions under which this growth has occurred, including the business climate and economic policy parameters, such as exchange rates. Figure 2.1 shows the comparative growth of manufacturing by world region.

The technological intensity of the majority of Vietnam's export goods is low (see chapter 1, figure 1.2, panel a). The share of high-technology goods is increasing, but at a slow rate. Indeed, the majority of exports use no technology at all. China, however, has successfully transitioned most of its export production into technology-intensive goods (chapter 1, figure 1.2, panel b).

The Slow Transformation to High Technology

China's economy, much like Vietnam's, was centrally planned. China used its wealth of cheap, unskilled labor to shift from a primarily agrarian society to the production of goods for export, also much like Vietnam. China now accounts for

Figure 2.1 Index of Manufacturing Value Added, by World Region, 1990–2010

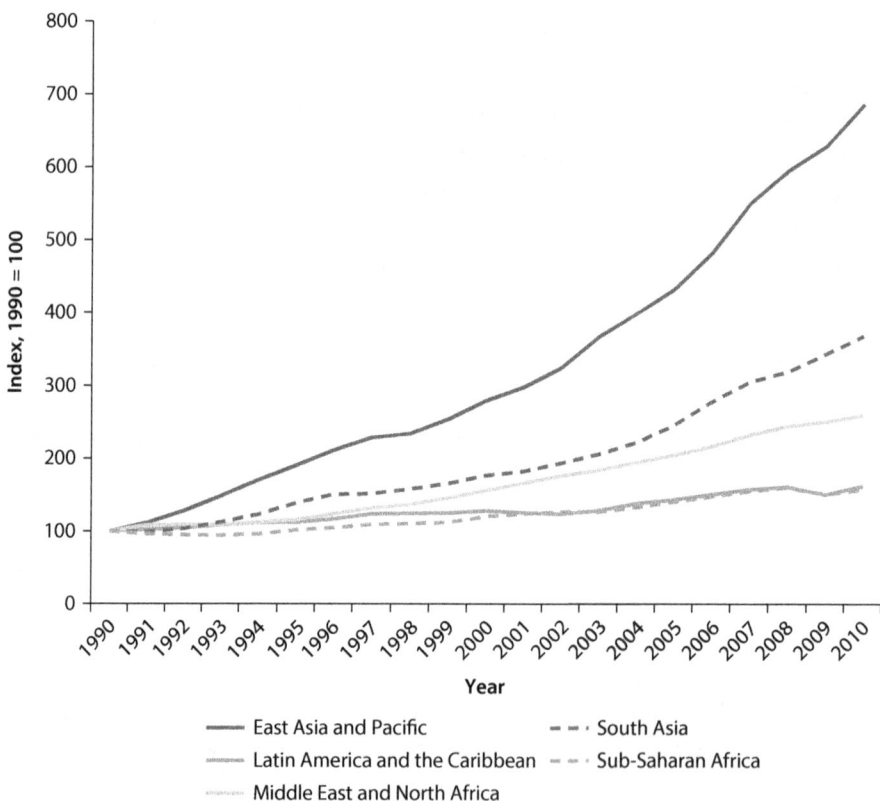

Source: World Bank 2012.

9 percent of global trade. While it is well known that Chinese reforms have been implemented in phases that began in the late 1970s, eight years before Vietnam's Doi Moi reforms, most of the early reforms in China were concerned with the decollectivization of agriculture in rural areas, which released a large number of surplus laborers for manufacturing (Dinh and others 2013). The reform process in Chinese manufacturing did not really begin until the late 1980s, when selected southern coastal provinces were opened to foreign investment—which succeeded in bringing investment, but also market links and managerial skills—and when private businesses in retailing and light industries were allowed in cities. Four cities in coastal south China—Shantou, Shenzhen, Xiamen, and Zhuhai—were chosen to host special economic zones to induce overseas investors to develop export-oriented manufacturing. These areas had a weak state-owned economy, but strong social links with overseas Chinese, who brought the first wave of foreign investment, mainly from Hong Kong SAR, China; Macao SAR, China; and Taiwan, China, and the associated links with markets overseas. Tariff reform was undertaken in the 1990s, but the pressure for change escalated when China sought accession to the World Trade Organization, which included negotiations on lower tariff rates and a removal of nontariff trading barriers affecting non-state entities.

Now dominant in the global market for light manufactures, China has transitioned its exports from primary products, such as gas, petroleum, live animals, and a few low-technology manufactures (for example, fabrics and footwear), to sophisticated medium- and high-technology products. The export share of the top 10 products in China's export basket did not shrink with the emergence of more light manufactures. Instead, it rose from 20.0 percent to 27.7 percent, reflecting the primacy of light and heavy manufactures (table 2.1). Footwear was the only major product that China exported in both the 1980s and the first decade of the 2000s.

By 2009, manufactured exports had grown to take up a 90 percent share of exports in China; they had risen to 58 percent in Vietnam. As China continues to diversify its export basket, it is moving to higher–value added, high-technology products. While table 2.1 exaggerates the sophistication of this export basket by including among the high-technology products many products that are only locally assembled and packaged, the fact that such goods are gaining importance does illustrate the ability of Chinese firms to fill the role of important providers along the product value chain, an ability Vietnamese firms must also seek.

The Comparative Productivity of China and Vietnam

We have chosen China as the benchmark for our in-depth study of the cost structure of production in light manufacturing in Vietnam because China is among the most competitive countries in the world in light manufacturing. China is a relevant comparator because, when it was emerging into world markets, it had to adapt profoundly to compete in the manufacture of goods that were then dominated by Hong Kong SAR, China; Korea; Singapore; and Taiwan, China.

Table 2.1 Top 10 Nonoil Exports, China, 1980–84 and 2004–08

1980–84			2004–08		
Product	Technology	Export share, %	Product	Technology	Export share, %
Woven, unbleached cotton fabrics	Low	3.1	Complete digital data processing machines	High	5.0
Gas, oils	Resource based	2.8	Peripheral control and adapter units	High	3.5
Linens, furnishings, textiles	Low	2.8	Parts and accessories	High	3.2
Woven, dyed cotton fabrics	Low	1.9	Television, radio broadcasting, and transmitters	High	3.1
Basketwork, brooms, paint rollers	Low	1.9	Machine parts and accessories	High	3.1
Footwear	Low	1.5	Footwear	Low	2.2
Woven and synthetic fiber fabrics	Medium	1.6	Sound recorders, video recorders	Medium	2.1
Outerwear and textiles, women and infants	Low	1.5	Electronic microcircuits	High	2.0
Fine animal hair, not carded or combed	Primary	1.5	Toys, indoor games, and so on	Low	1.9
Swine, live	Primary	1.5	Knitted and crocheted outerwear	Low	1.9
Total share		20.1	Total share		28.0

Source: Dinh and others 2012.

Certainly, the initial conditions under which China and Vietnam embarked on the path to development were different. Moreover, each country has unique resource endowments and particular comparative advantages. Nonetheless, light manufacturing products made in Vietnam will have to compete with products made in China. For this reason, we must understand clearly what would be required if Vietnam is to seize and retain a significant market share in light manufacturing products.

Table 2.2 highlights the sources of growth in gross domestic product (GDP) in each country in 1990–2008. It shows that growth in Vietnam has relied on capital more than on productivity, whereas reliance on productivity has been the hallmark in China's growth. Total factor productivity captures the efficiency of factor inputs in the production process, and, as indicated in the table, while China has demonstrated high total factor productivity over the past decade, there has been a significant decline in Vietnam, where the accumulation of capital, rather than the efficient use of capital, has been the main driver of growth. Total factor productivity accounted for 44 percent of Vietnam's GDP growth in the 1990s, but the share then declined to 26 percent in 2000–08. During the same period, the contribution of capital increased from 35 percent to 53 percent. In China, in contrast, the contribution of total factor productivity to economic growth was above 50 percent.

Figure 2.2 plots the evolution in productivity in the two countries over 2000–12. The productivity gap between China and Vietnam is large and, without policy reforms in Vietnam, will widen.

An alternative systemic explanation focuses on policy-driven changes in real wages relative to productivity. Labor productivity plays an important role in the prosperity of an economy because it is related closely to wages.

Table 2.2 Sources of GDP Growth, China and Vietnam, 1990–2008

Country	1990–2000				2000–08			
	GDP growth	Sources of growth			GDP growth	Sources of growth		
		Capital	Labor	TFP		Capital	Labor	TFP
Contribution, percentage points per year								
Vietnam	7.2	2.5	1.6	3.2	7.3	3.9	1.4	1.9
China	9.9	3.6	0.7	5.5	9.7	4.1	0.6	5.0
Contribution, share								
Vietnam	100.0	34.7	22.2	44.4	100.0	53.4	19.2	26.0
China	100.0	36.4	7.1	55.6	100.0	42.3	6.2	51.5

Source: Ketels and others 2010.
Note: GDP = gross domestic product; TFP = total factor productivity, which measures efficiency in the use of capital and labor.

Figure 2.2 Productivity Growth, China and Vietnam, 2000–12

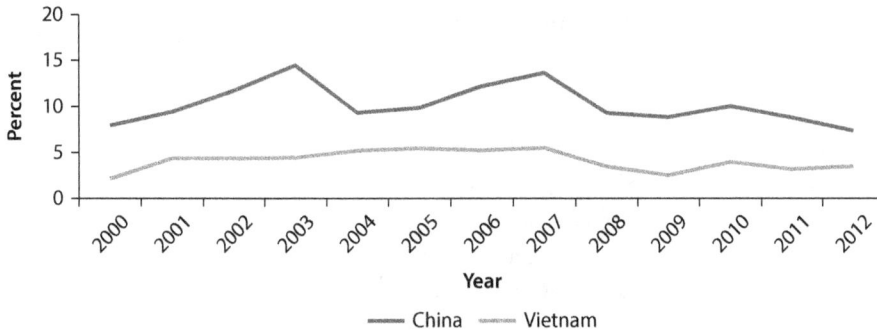

Source: Total Economy Database, Conference Board, New York, http://www.conference-board.org/data/economydatabase.

Labor productivity in Vietnam has increased an average of 4.2 percent a year, but this is considerably lower than China's 10.3 percent. In absolute terms, Vietnam's labor productivity ($5,871) is about 46 percent of China's labor productivity ($12,641). The results of a comparison of manufacturing sector productivity are similar. In the manufacture of polo shirts, for instance, Vietnam's labor productivity (12 pieces per day) is not even half China's (25 pieces) (see below).

At prevailing exchange rates, the U.S. dollar values of skilled and unskilled wages in China have now risen well above those in Vietnam in the five product areas we examine in our study. Skilled wages in Vietnam are 55 percent of skilled wages in China, while unskilled wages in Vietnam are 43 percent of the corresponding wages in China. The implication—qualified because of the small sample size—is that real wages in Vietnam are actually or potentially competitive (subject to productivity levels), and, if Vietnam plays it right, it could capture a much larger export share in the global market.

Table 2.3 shows how wages in a variety of light manufacturing subsectors in Vietnam compare with the corresponding wages in China and Ethiopia, which is similar in size to Vietnam.

Table 2.3 Average Monthly Wages in Selected Subsectors, China, Ethiopia, and Vietnam, 2010

U.S. dollars

Product	Labor type	China	Vietnam	Ethiopia
Polo shirts	Skilled	311–370	119–181	37–185
Dairy milk	Skilled	177–206	—	30–63
Wood chairs	Skilled	383–442	181–259	81–119
Crown corks	Skilled	265–369	168–233	181–
Leather loafers	Skilled	296–562	119–140	41–96
Milled wheat	Skilled	398–442	181–363	89–141
Average	**Skilled**	**305–399**	**154–235**	**77–131**
Polo shirts	Unskilled	237–296	78–130	26–48
Dairy milk	Unskilled	118–133	31–78	13–41
Wood chairs	Unskilled	206–251	85–135	37–52
Crown corks	Unskilled	192–265	117–142	89–
Leather loafers	Unskilled	237–488	78–93	16–33
Milled wheat	Unskilled	192–236	78–207	26–52
Average	**Unskilled**	**197–278**	**78–131**	**35–53**

Source: GDS 2011.

Note: The upper value for crown corks (bottle caps) is not available for Ethiopia; — = not available.

These data refer to the cash wages paid to factory workers. Labor costs, not limited to cash wages, include employer contributions to pension plans, health and unemployment insurance, and other fringe benefits, as well as employer outlays on training, housing, recreation, and so on.

A low-wage advantage alone does not guarantee Vietnam a comparative advantage in less-skilled, labor-intensive manufacturing. Because Vietnam competes with other low-wage regions (for example, South Asia and Africa), at least two other factors come into play. First, productivity is as important as wages in determining comparative advantage. Second, because wages and labor productivity vary across sectors, sector specificity is an important determinant of a country's comparative advantage in labor-intensive light manufacturing.

The Overall Business Environment

The competitiveness of Vietnamese producers is affected by the country's conditions for doing business (table 2.4). The critical areas include protecting investors, getting electricity, resolving insolvency, the issue of onerous taxation, and business start-up policies and practices.

The World Bank's doing business rankings should be considered together with the World Economic Forum's global competitiveness rankings. Both reflect the business environment outside factories. The latter indicator shows Vietnam at 75th and China at 29th.[2] A recent World Bank report also points out that trade facilitation and logistics in Vietnam need substantial improvement if the country is to become more export competitive (Pham and others 2013).

Table 2.4 Doing Business and Global Competitiveness Rankings, China and Vietnam, 2013

	China	Vietnam
Doing business	91	99
Global competitiveness	29	75

Sources: Schwab 2012; World Bank and IFC 2012.

In-Factory Productivity

Possible explanations of the poor within-factory competitiveness in Vietnam include the low levels of and lack of improvement in labor efficiency (for example, because of inadequate skilled labor and motivation) and low production efficiency (high utility use), both of which are documented in the value chain study discussed in detail in other chapters. Technical efficiency (or inefficiency) can be indicated by the amount of waste, product rejection rates, labor absenteeism, and poor capacity use (see the benchmarking key variable tables in chapters 4–8).

China's Growing Labor Cost Disadvantage: An Opportunity

Vietnam could become an early beneficiary of the associated structural changes if China acts to rebalance its economy by increasing domestic consumption and reducing the trade surplus caused by rising real wages, while permitting the real yuan rate to appreciate. Chinese products have penetrated almost every corner of the global market. China supplied 18 percent of the total value of combined European Union–United States market imports in 2004 and 35 percent in 2008. However, the capacity of Chinese coastal firms to outperform rivals in low-income countries in price and quality in light industry manufactures has begun to decline. The depletion of China's large pool of less-skilled workers and rapid cost increases, particularly in wages and nonwage labor expenses, are pricing growing numbers of coastal export firms in China out of the global markets for an expanding array of labor-intensive light industrial products.

Rising wages, the enforcement of stiffening labor and environmental regulations, the gradual expansion of costly safety net provisions, and the prospect of additional increases in the international value of the yuan mean that the erosion of China's comparative advantage in the export of labor-intensive manufactures will continue and perhaps accelerate (figure 2.3). This represents an opportunity for Vietnam to fill a portion of the widening gap in the supply of export products.

The Implications for Vietnamese Industries

To enhance competitiveness, favorable changes must take place at the micro (factory, sectoral, and macro levels. Changes at the macro level are discussed elsewhere (Thai and Dinh 2011). This volume examines sectoral and micro changes, including how these changes may occur and what conditions would be required to implement them.

Figure 2.3 Rising Labor Productivity and Wages in Manufacturing, China, 1979–2007

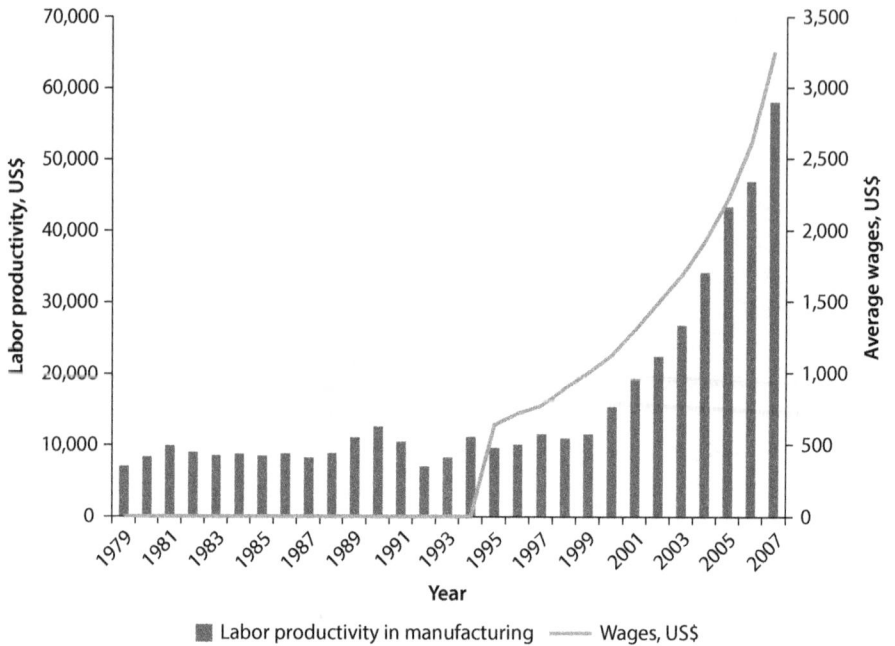

Source: Industrial Statistics Database, United Nations Industrial Development Organization, Vienna, http://www.unido.org
/resources/statistics/statistical-databases.html; NBS 2010.

The Main Constraints on Light Manufacturing

Vietnam has performed reasonably well in light manufacturing over the last two decades. The average annual growth of production has exceeded 10 percent a year, and the sector now accounts for 25 percent of GDP. There were more than 415,600 firms in the sector in 2009.

Nonetheless, the sector still suffers from a number of problems. We first list these problems and then examine them in subsections. Along the way, we compare the situation in Vietnam with the situation in our benchmark country, China.

Based on the surveys conducted by the study team, our list of problems in light manufacturing in Vietnam is as follows:

• Growth in light manufacturing has come from the sheer number of micro and small enterprises rather than from a growing number of medium and large firms. Each year, a great many enterprises disappear, and as many or more enter into production. Few of these micro and small enterprises ever reach medium size, creating a missing middle phenomenon common in developing countries. The problem with this pattern of growth is that these micro and small enterprises are engaged in low-productivity domestic production activities and have no access to modern technology and knowledge. This is why overall labor productivity is lower in Vietnam than in China, although the Vietnamese workers in foreign-invested companies are as productive as any workers in the world.

- There is a dualism in Vietnam: on the one side are low-productivity domestic enterprises; on the other are high-productivity enterprises supported by foreign direct investment (FDI) that produce for export and in which production is based on modern methods and technology. These foreign-invested firms are generally large (employing more than 1,000 workers), have a relatively small profit margin (10–15 percent or less), and do not produce for the domestic market. In contrast, firms producing for the domestic market are generally small and numerous. Some enjoy a good profit margin (20–30 percent), and most have few links to larger firms.

- There is little value chain integration in the production process. The large firms producing for export generally obtain raw materials and intermediate goods from abroad, while domestic firms buy from a variety of sources, including traders. There are few interactions between these two types of firms, unlike in China, where subcontracting between large and small firms is common.

- As a result of this production structure (a large number of small household enterprises producing for the domestic market operate alongside a small number of modern, foreign-invested enterprises producing for export, with few links between the two types), Vietnam's rapid economic growth over the last 20 years has not resulted in or been accompanied by a trade surplus. Indeed, the widening trade deficit—11.0 percent of GDP in 2009, but only 3.5 percent five years earlier—has continued to threaten macroeconomic stability. Because the deficit has an effect on manufacturing growth, it is a key component in a vicious circle.

- This structure of production, which may have been suitable when Vietnam began to open up, is unlikely to sustain future industrial growth and, more importantly, will not support the country's effort to become industrialized. The manufacturing sector depends on an efficient foreign-invested industry that relies on a small profit margin, cheap and low-skilled labor, and imports of raw materials and intermediate goods, with few or no links to the domestic market, which is dominated by numerous small enterprises using low-productivity methods and often outdated technology to supply goods. Many of the foreign-invested industries would likely move production elsewhere should real wages rise in Vietnam, wiping out all the country's hard-earned gains over the last two decades. For domestic industries, the lack of economies of scale and the insufficient competition from imports mean that they are not motivated to adopt new production methods and technologies.

- Existing industrial policies appear to support the birth, but not the growth of small and medium enterprises (SMEs). Unlike China, Vietnam has not attempted to promote medium and large enterprises. The dearth of large domestic enterprises means that the numerous micro and small enterprises have not been able to benefit from subcontracting by large enterprises, which, likewise, do not draw on the competitive production of smaller enterprises.

- Ultimately, if micro and small enterprises are to grow into medium and large enterprises, the role of state-owned enterprises (SOEs) needs to be reassessed. The report uses a definition of SOEs that is different from the one prevalent in Vietnam. An SOE is an enterprise that is owned directly or indirectly by the state. An enterprise is private only if it is owned 100 percent by the private sector. According to our definition, SOEs in Vietnam are still prevalent in the manufacturing sector, particularly in the garment industry, a situation that stands in contrast to China. Besides placing private enterprises at a disadvantage, the large presence of SOEs also discourages micro and small enterprises from growing because the latter fear that the competition with SOEs could be detrimental. Because of the distorted incentives, SOEs consume resources in finance and administration that would otherwise be available to help small private enterprises grow.

- There are areas in which the government needs to be involved, but is currently absent. There are also areas in which the government is currently active, but should not be. The SOEs are a clear example of the latter, whereas the need to compile and disseminate information to help SME entrepreneurs is an example of the former. As China's case renders evident, the government's role in establishing plug-and-play industrial parks and input and output markets, providing cheap land, and guiding the growth of organic clusters into industrial zones is crucial if small enterprises are to become larger (Dinh and others 2013).

We examine five key sectors below and in subsequent chapters: apparel, leather, wood products, metal products, and agribusiness. These five sectors are the key foreign exchange earners in the country. The exports of these sectors account for about 40 percent of total commodity exports.

A number of important characteristics of light manufacturing are analyzed in the following subsections: labor characteristics, the size distribution of firms, the preponderance of SOEs, the weak integration into the value chain, problems in access to finance, and the lack of government support.

Labor Characteristics

Of the five sectors, agribusiness, apparel, and leather provide the most employment, and leather is the most labor intensive. Apparel production employs more women than any of the other five sectors, and leather is not far behind. The dominance of women in sectors such as apparel and leather has important implications for development because of the role women play in households.[3]

In China, Ethiopia, Tanzania, Vietnam, and Zambia, the five countries examined in detail in the quantitative survey undertaken by our study team, the share

Table 2.5 Workforce by Occupational Category, China, Ethiopia, and Vietnam, 2009/10–2010/11

Percent

Occupational breakdown	China		Vietnam		Ethiopia	
	2010/11	*2009/10*	*2010/11*	*2009/10*	*2010/11*	*2009/10*
Total production workers	73	75	81	81	73	73
Skilled	46	47	62	61	58	58
Unskilled	27	28	19	19	15	15
Management	16	14	4	3	23	23
Clerical and other	10	10	16	16	4	3
Number of observations	255	226	299	296	249	205

Source: Fafchamps and Quinn 2012.

of production workers among all workers is largest in Vietnam (Fafchamps and Quinn 2012). Moreover, Vietnam has the largest share of skilled production workers, while China has a larger share of management workers than Vietnam. Table 2.5 shows the share of workers in four broad occupational categories during the year of the survey (2010/11) and the previous year. Skilled and unskilled production workers physically produce output. However, a firm cannot operate efficiently without management and clerical workers. Given that the firms we are studying are all involved in manufacturing, labor productivity would be maximized, in theory, if the number of management and clerical workers were kept to a minimum. The extent to which firms can minimize the size of the management and clerical workforce, however, depends on the ease with which production workers can be organized and monitored. In turn, this depends on the educational attainment of the workforce (for example, whether workers can read written instructions) and on social norms of discipline and effort. The less well disciplined and less well educated the workforce is, the greater the need for workers who monitor and process information, and, thus, the larger the share of management and clerical workers in the total workforce.

The educational attainment and experience of entry-level production workers are lower in Vietnam than in China. In figure 2.4, we report the cumulative distribution of the average educational level of new production workers in each of the three countries. The lower the curve, the higher the educational attainment of workers. China has the lowest curve overall, indicating that its workforce is generally more well educated than production workers in the other countries. In China and Vietnam, only a small proportion of production workers have less than nine years of schooling. This probably reflects differences in legislation on compulsory schooling in past decades.

The Size Distribution of Firms
Micro and Small Businesses: A Dominating Share in all Five Sectors
In 2011, approximately 25,500, or 8 percent, of the active enterprises in Vietnam were operating in the five sectors. This included private domestic enterprises, foreign-invested firms, and SOEs.[4] The five sectors accounted for 2.7 million

Figure 2.4 Years of Schooling among New Production Workers, China, Ethiopia, and Vietnam, 2010

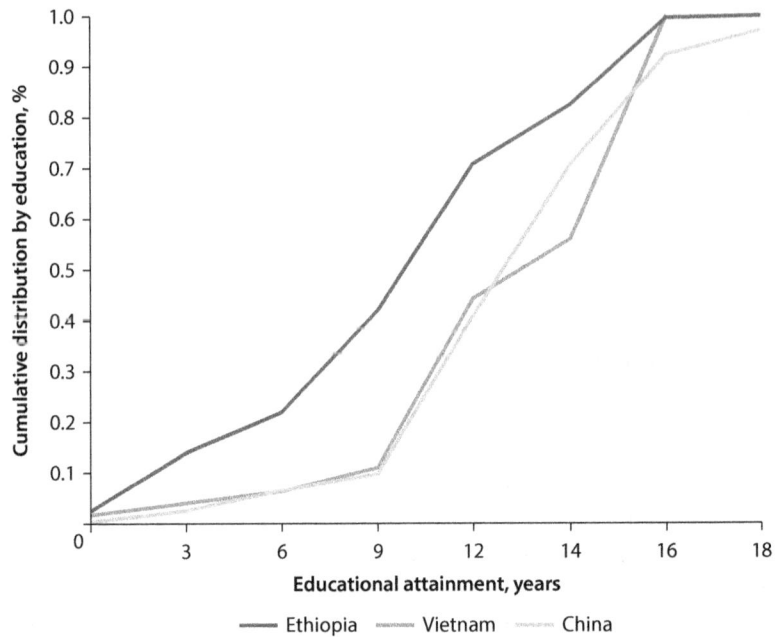

Source: Fafchamps and Quinn 2012.
Note: The figure shows the cumulative distribution of the average educational level of new production workers.

jobs, 68 percent of which were held by women. Apparel, leather and shoes, and agribusiness are the major job suppliers. There are few large private domestic enterprises in the five sectors. The number of medium domestic enterprises that have the potential to become larger is limited. This is one of Vietnam's most critical problems because firms are unable to leverage economies of scale; invest in research and development, technology, and product design; or move up the value added ladder in these sectors.

An overwhelming number of new enterprises have been established since 2000, but the vast majority are small (figure 2.5). This lopsided development and size disparity severely limit the potential of enterprises individually and the economy as a whole. Additionally, almost all large enterprises are foreign or state owned, while the majority of privately owned firms are small.

Across the five sectors, few enterprises have more than $10 million in capital. Enterprises that can reach $30 million in capital are even fewer.

Several reasons explain why the government's priority should be on facilitating the growth of small firms to medium firms and the growth of medium firms to large firms rather than on the creation of so many small companies that go out of business year after year. First, given the structure of Vietnamese industry, low productivity growth in the economy is associated with the large number of micro and household enterprises. Moreover, while large and foreign-invested enterprises have integrated into the world market through international trade,

Figure 2.5 Size Distribution of Manufacturing Firms, Vietnam, 2000 and 2011

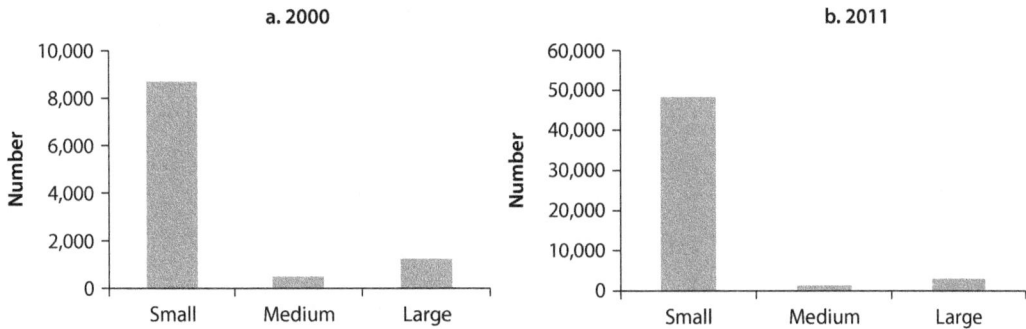

Source: GSO 2013.

the micro and household enterprises produce mainly for the domestic market, are insulated from foreign technology and demand, and concentrate on low-productivity activities. This reflects the preponderant evidence from around the world that shows that labor productivity is much lower in smaller firms than in larger firms.

Second, Vietnam is now at a stage of industrial development where it is more important to shift to higher–value added activities rather than the mere growth of SMEs, which the country had to rely on during the initial phase of the development of light manufacturing. Shifting to higher–value added, higher-productivity activities requires more capital intensity, more skills, and a larger scale than micro and household enterprises are capable of generating, particularly in terms of the creation of strong national brands or the introduction of new, cost-effective technologies.

Third, the appearance and disappearance of a large number of enterprises year after year entail a cost to the economy that can be avoided.

This is not to say that SMEs should be discouraged. Vietnam can grow according to a model in which SMEs represent the backbone of the economy (as in Taiwan, China) or a model in which large companies are the dominant players (as in Korea). No matter which model is followed, the key issue is to raise the productivity of micro, small, and household enterprises by integrating them into the value chain of the domestic economy and the international economy. Only then can the country achieve significant and sustainable economic growth.

Possible Reasons for the Dual Industrial Structure

The majority of enterprises employ fewer than 500 workers. Firms employing fewer than 50 workers account for the dominant share, especially in metal products, wood products, and food processing (table 2.6).

There are many reasons why small enterprises fail to become medium enterprises. One is the unclear government policy toward the private sector. The overall policy is to promote private enterprise, but it is silent about promoting large private enterprises, which could become engines of growth in the five sectors or across the entire economy.

Table 2.6 Size of Enterprises, by Number of Employees, Five Sectors, Vietnam, 2011

Indicator	Food and beverage processing	Garments	Metal products	Wood	Leather and shoes
Firms, total	7,466	4,654	8,223	3,878	1,260
Firms, by number of employees, %					
Fewer than 50	77.7	61.2	89.2	86.0	49.9
50–499	18.9	28.5	10.2	13.5	33.4
500 or more	3.4	10.3	0.6	0.5	16.7

Source: GSO 2013.

Meanwhile, SOEs in many sectors see competition increasing from private enterprises and are afraid of losing their market share. There have been reports of SOEs interfering to prevent entry into the market or to slow the growth of private enterprises operating in their sectors.

The policy approach has created a dual industrial structure: a large number of small, household enterprises producing for the domestic market and a small number of modern, foreign-invested enterprises producing for export. The household enterprises engage in low-productivity activities and have few connections with the modern economy. Most of these household enterprises are in the informal sector, and they operate separately from the large or higher-end tradable goods markets, pay little in taxes, and are not affected by the formal regulations that affect formal enterprises. At the end of 2010, according to an estimate of the Vietnamese Chamber of Commerce and Industry, there were 1 million household businesses in the semi-informal sector that were registered and paid taxes at the district level and another 3 million household enterprises that were not registered in any way, compared with about 544,000 formal sector firms (including private firms, SOEs, and foreign-invested enterprises), of which only about 65 percent were active (Phạm 2012).

There are a number of reasons why the size distribution of firms in Vietnam differs from that of firms in more advanced countries. First, in Vietnam, the preponderance of SOEs discourages private sector firms from growing (see below). Second, the lack of an explicit public policy to promote medium and large private firms compounds this ambiguity. Third, firms stay small to avoid the high cost of doing business, including taxes, the regulatory burden, and bribes. Finally, as Dinh, Mavridis, and Nguyen (2012) show, limited access to financing can skew the distribution by increasing the share of small firms. Vietnam's industrial structure may therefore be a direct result of the country's limited financial development and lower domestic savings relative to countries in other regions.

As a result of the lack of competitiveness, Vietnam's domestically produced goods face tough import competition, mainly from China. The recent real wage increases in China have only slightly reduced the pressures from Chinese imports, while the level of imports into Vietnam from other countries in the Association of Southeast Asian Nations may rise. This will create difficulties in the balance of trade (see above).

The Dominance of SOEs

The *Vietnam Development Report 2012* notes that, while the number of SOEs has fallen by about half over the last 10 years, SOEs have nonetheless maintained a dominant role in the economy (World Bank 2011). Among the 200 largest enterprises in 2007, a mere 22 were private (Cheshier and Penrose 2007). Thus, the majority of large companies in Vietnam are either SOEs or foreign-owned enterprises.

SOEs generally appear to perform well. However, this is misleading because the performance should be much better given the advantages of SOEs relative to the private sector. First, the government allocates or leases land at a fixed rate to SOEs for long periods. Some SOEs even obtain surplus land to lease to others, which provides income that can help offset losses incurred through other business activities. Second, SOEs receive preferential treatment in the access to credit. For example, under certain circumstances, SOEs do not have to apply for loans through banks; they can gain access to loans at low rates through the government or through official development assistance. In contrast, private companies must pay high interest rates, which lead to higher production costs.

Nonetheless, the number of SOEs fell by nearly half over 2000–11 (table 2.7). There is evidence that this decline was accompanied by growth in the share of private domestic companies in industrial output. Over 2000–07, the share of private firms grew from 9.8 percent to 24.3 percent, a nearly 150 percent increase, largely at the expense of SOEs (Taussig 2009). This underlines the fact that private domestic and foreign-invested enterprises have taken advantage of the decline in SOEs to become more active.

However, despite the rapid equitization of SOEs in the 1990s and the first decade of the 2000s, there has actually been an increase in the number of SOEs in recent years. Indeed, 175 were added in 2009. Even though thousands of enterprises are transitioning into privately owned firms, this recent increase reminds us that SOEs are still active and important in Vietnam. Indeed, the decline in the number of SOEs is not obvious in the number of employees (table 2.8). Moreover, despite the decline in the share of the state-owned sector in terms of fixed assets and total profits, SOEs are still significant players in the economy, accounting for about 40 percent of GDP. In addition, they remain noteworthy because each is so large and because of the nature of the products they supply. For example, the SOEs controlled by the central government

Table 2.7 Number of Enterprises, by Type, Vietnam, 2000 and 2011

Enterprise type	2000	2011
SOEs controlled by the central government	2,067	1,797
SOEs managed by local governments	3,692	1,468
Collectives	3,237	13,338
Private enterprises	20,548	312,416
Foreign-owned enterprises	1,525	9,010

Source: GSO 2013.
Note: SOE = state-owned enterprise.

Table 2.8 Indicators of the Size of Enterprises, by Type, Vietnam, 2005–11

Indicator, average	Private SMEs		SOEs		Foreign-invested firms	
	2005	2011	2005	2011	2005	2011
Net turnover per enterprise, $, millions	6,089	17,842	77,214	825,624	106,201	225,534
Employees per enterprise, number	27	21	363	510	267	283
Turnover per employee, $, millions	225.3	834.4	212.9	1,619.6	397.4	796.7

Source: GSO 2013.
Note: SME = small and medium enterprise; SOE = state-owned enterprise.

include enterprises that provide public utilities, such as electricity and telecommunications (Ishizuka 2011). The majority of these central SOEs still exist, though the number declined by about 13 percent over 2000–11 (see table 2.7). Furthermore, SOEs have control over certain products, allowing them to raise prices without the risk of losing customers. Major commercial sectors, as well as consumer goods, are dominated by SOEs. Goods and services, such as fertilizer, telecommunications, and beer production, are controlled by the state. If a single SOE cannot achieve a monopoly over the market, SOEs will work together in groups favored by the government—these groups are known as state economic groups—to fix prices (see below). In these situations, there is little room for competition and little need for higher productivity and innovation.

This level of state involvement is worrisome. Historically, no economy has achieved rapid growth without a strong private sector. The Chinese economy, for example, did not take off until the early 1990s when private initiatives became established. SOEs in China are now practically nonexistent in the light manufacturing sector. Similarly, SOEs in Vietnam need to pull back in crucial areas and allow the private sector to respond to market incentives.

Foreign-Owned Enterprises

In Vietnam, most of the largest companies that are not SOEs are foreign owned. These enterprises capitalize on Vietnam's low-wage labor cost advantage, in conjunction with (directly) imported inputs, to produce goods and export them across the globe. More than half of Vietnamese exports are produced by foreign-owned enterprises (table 2.9). These firms are not integrated into the rest of the economy, to which they transfer little knowledge or technology. Over 2000–11, the number of foreign-owned enterprises increased sixfold, generating more employment in the domestic economy (see table 2.7).

Foreign-owned enterprises are having much greater success than domestic producers, highlighting the need for Vietnamese firms to harness the expertise to produce goods at the same level of productivity and rapid pace. This also underscores the issue of employment generation, which will shift to other countries if Vietnam loses its wage competitiveness.

Private Sector SMEs

The number of private sector SMEs continues to grow, but, in terms of productivity, they still lag behind SOEs and foreign-invested firms. This is evident in the

Table 2.9 Exports of Goods and Services, by Economic Sector, Vietnam, 2007–12

Indicator	2007	2008	2009	2010	2011	2012[a]
Total exports, $, millions	48,561	62,685	57,096	72,236	96,905	114,529
Domestic economic sector, %	43	45	47	46	43	37
Foreign direct–invested sector, %	57	55	53	54	57	63

Source: GSO 2013.
a. The data for 2012 are preliminary.

average turnover per employee, for example (see table 2.8). The sheer size of SOEs and foreign-invested firms relative to SMEs is also noteworthy. The missing middle is an obstacle to the competition of SMEs with such large and powerful corporations and to the full realization of the potential of SMEs.

The lack of medium enterprises has proven challenging in the efforts of private SMEs to bridge the missing middle and grow into larger corporations or create international brands. The majority of firms have fewer than 20 employees, mainly family members who assume multiple, ill-defined roles. These family firms embody a survival mentality rather than a focus on productivity and growth.

The Weak Links between Domestic SMEs and Foreign-Invested Enterprises and SOEs

In seeking to meet their business needs, foreign-invested enterprises and SOEs avoid relying on small private sector enterprises. The transfer of technology and knowledge between foreign-invested enterprises and domestic enterprises is negligible. Larger enterprises do not depend on inputs produced by their smaller domestic counterparts. Instead, they import raw materials, while domestic firms buy from a variety of sources, including trading companies. SOEs, which are supposed to play a leading role in key industries (for example, in logistics, machinery and equipment, and chemicals), are unable to provide key inputs to manufacturing enterprises in the five sectors.

This fragmentation and lack of interaction are problematic because they limit the ability to source inputs, new technologies, expertise, and so on domestically, preventing the economy from becoming more productive. Additionally, time, effort, and foreign exchange could be saved by greater integration among firms, which would also spur other economic benefits and greater local growth.

Access to Finance[5]

In Vietnam, as well as in China and other developing countries, few SMEs seek start-up capital from banks. Even if they do, their requests are rarely granted. Instead, SMEs rely on their own savings or other informal sources, such as the savings of family members and friends. The difference between China and other countries is that, in China, banks play an important role in helping those SMEs that have survived the first few years to expand, especially through assistance in the purchase of capital equipment or land.

Fafchamps and Quinn (2012) report that the terms of loans tend to differ across the five countries studied. There are also differences in collateral requirements and average interest rates. Even after controlling for firm size, they find that Chinese firms face substantially lower average collateral requirements. Similarly, Chinese firms pay an average annual interest rate of about 4.7 percent, compared with average annual interest rates of about 10 percent in Ethiopia and 14 percent in Vietnam (the survey was conducted in late 2010). These proportions change little across the firm-size distribution. The differences cannot be explained merely by differences in the information available to lenders.

Substantially lower collateral requirements reduce the total costs to the lender; this may explain why Chinese banks are more likely to lend to manufacturers and charge lower interest rates. It may also be that many Chinese firms are located in industrial zones, where collateral requirements are less demanding, or it may be that Chinese banks, many of which are owned by the government, have been instructed to lend to manufacturers at low interest rates and without burdensome collateral requirements.

Little Government Support for the Five Sectors

Most of Vietnam's private enterprises are growing without direct government support. All the enterprise representatives we interviewed, except for the representatives of SOEs, said they received no direct support from the government. However, many also agreed that the government had adopted some measures to accelerate growth in the five sectors. These measures include encouraging foreign direct investment among industries, liberalizing regulations on private sector start-ups, liberalizing trade, and carrying out limited SOE reforms, albeit at an uneven pace.[6] In the five sectors in our study, SOE reforms have been deeper in the wood and leather sectors. In the leather sector, all SOEs have been equitized (but not completely privatized). In the garment, food processing, and metal product sectors, many large SOEs are still competing with private enterprises. SOEs are also one of the factors impeding the scaling-up of private SMEs in the sectors because of unfair competition and the absolute advantages of SOEs in accessing scarce resources such as land, credit, and opportunities for market information. More profound reforms of SOEs in these sectors, in which the government should not play a leading role, are needed to enhance the development of private SMEs and to promote the greater competitiveness of the industries as a whole.

Notes

1. We use the broad definition of light manufacturing here, which includes the transformation of agricultural products (agribusiness).

2. See the separate country economic profiles in Schwab (2012) for definitions.

3. Women are more family oriented than men in that they tend to spend a greater proportion of their income on household consumption goods, especially for their children. This is particularly true of food, and food and nutrition have underlying consequences in development.

4. There were 630,000 enterprises registered as of the end of 2011. However, the General Statistics Office survey in that year disclosed that only 324,690 were active (GSO 2012).

5. This subsection is based on Fafchamps and Quinn (2012).

6. Before 1991, private business was not allowed. Between 1991 and 1999, private business was allowed, but market entry was extremely costly and difficult. The Enterprise Law of 1999 liberalized the regulation of private entrepreneurship, and the 2004 Investment Law unified domestic and export companies. By the end of 2009, 415,591 enterprises had been registered across the country. There are now nearly 20,000 enterprises operating in the five sectors. The growth of these sectors would not have been possible without the new legal regime.

References

Cheshier, Scott, and Jago Penrose. 2007. "Top 200: Industrial Strategies of Viet Nam's Largest Firms." October, United Nations Development Programme, Hanoi.

Dinh, Hinh T., Dimitris A. Mavridis, and Hoa B. Nguyen. 2012. "The Binding Constraint on the Growth of Firms in Developing Countries." In *Performance of Manufacturing Firms in Africa: An Empirical Analysis*, edited by Hinh T. Dinh and George R. G. Clarke, 87–137. Washington, DC: World Bank.

Dinh, Hinh T., Vincent Palmade, Vandana Chandra, and Frances Cossar. 2012. *Light Manufacturing in Africa: Targeted Policies to Enhance Private Investment and Create Jobs.* Washington, DC: World Bank. http://go.worldbank.org/ASG0J44350.

Dinh, Hinh T., Thomas G. Rawski, Ali Zafar, Lihong Wang, and Eleonora Mavroeidi. 2013. *Tales from the Development Frontier: How China and Other Countries Harness Light Manufacturing to Create Jobs and Prosperity.* With Xin Tong and Pengfei Li. Washington, DC: World Bank.

Fafchamps, Marcel, and Simon Quinn. 2012. "Results of Sample Surveys of Firms." In *Performance of Manufacturing Firms in Africa: An Empirical Analysis*, edited by Hinh T. Dinh and George R. G. Clarke, 139–211. Washington, DC: World Bank.

GDS (Global Development Solutions). 2011. *The Value Chain and Feasibility Analysis; Domestic Resource Cost Analysis.* Vol. 2 of *Light Manufacturing in Africa: Targeted Policies to Enhance Private Investment and Create Jobs.* Washington, DC: World Bank. http://go.worldbank.org/6G2A3TFI20.

GSO (General Statistics Office of Vietnam). 2012. *Statistical Yearbook of Vietnam 2012.* Hanoi: GSO.

———. 2013. *Statistical Yearbook of Vietnam 2013.* Hanoi: GSO.

Ishizuka, Futaba. 2011. "Economic Restructuring and Regional Distribution of Enterprises in Vietnam." IDE Discussion Paper 293, Institute of Developing Economies, Japan External Trade Organization, Chiba, Japan. http://www.ide.go.jp/English/Publish/Download/Dp/pdf/293.pdf.

Ketels, Christian, Nguyen Dinh Cung, Nguyen Thi Tue Anh, and Do Hong Hanh. 2010. *Vietnam Competitiveness Report 2010.* Singapore: Asia Competitiveness Institute, Lee Kuan Yew School of Public Policy, National University of Singapore. http://www.isc.hbs.edu/pdf/Vietnam_Competitiveness_Report_2010_Eng.pdf.

NBS (National Bureau of Statistics of China). 2010. *China Statistical Yearbook 2010.* Beijing: China Statistics Press. http://www.stats.gov.cn/tjsj/ndsj/2010/indexeh.htm.

Pham, Duc Minh, Deepak Mishra, Kee-Cheok Cheong, John Arnold, Anh Minh Trinh, Huyen Thi Ngoc Ngo, and Hien Thi Phuong Nguyen. 2013. *Trade Facilitation, Value Creation, and Competitiveness: Policy Implications for Vietnam's Economic Growth.* Vol. 1. Hanoi: World Bank.

Phạm Thị Thu Hằng. 2012. "Quan Hệ Giữa Cải Cách DNNN và Sự Phát Triển Của Khu Vực Tư Nhân: Thực Trạng Và Những Vấn Đề Đặt Ra." [Relations between SOE reforms and private sector development: Facts and outstanding issues]. [In Vietnamese.] Vietnam Chamber of Commerce, Hanoi.

Schwab, Klaus, ed. 2012. *Insight Report: The Global Competitiveness Report 2012–2013.* Geneva: World Economic Forum.

Taussig, Markus. 2009. "Business Strategy during Radical Economic Transition: Vietnam's First Generation of Large Private Manufacturers and a Decade of Intensifying Opportunities and Competition." Policy Discussion Paper, United Nations Development Programme, Hanoi. http://www.undp.org.vn/digitalAssets/19/19020 _Business_strategies_during_radical_economic_transition-final.pdf.

Thai, Van Can, and Hinh T. Dinh. 2011. "Towards a Credible Economic Program to Achieve High and Sustainable Economic Growth." Policy Discussion Paper 02, Center for Economic and Policy Research, University of Economics and Business, Vietnam National University, Hanoi.

World Bank. 2011. *Vietnam Development Report 2012: Market Economy for a Middle-Income Vietnam.* Joint Donor Report to the Vietnam Consultative Group Meeting, Hanoi. http://www-wds.worldbank.org/external/default/WDSContentServer/WDSP/IB/2011 /12/13/000333037_20111213003843/Rendered/PDF/659800AR00PUBL0elopment0 Report02012.pdf.

———. 2012. *World Development Indicators 2012.* April. Washington, DC: World Bank. http://data.worldbank.org/sites/default/files/wdi-2012-ebook.pdf.

World Bank and IFC (International Finance Corporation). 2012. *Doing Business 2013: Smarter Regulations for Small and Medium-Size Enterprises.* Washington, DC: World Bank. http://www.doingbusiness.org/reports/global-reports/doing -business-2013.

CHAPTER 3

Strengthening Light Manufacturing

Vietnam's Potential

Several factors have enlarged the markets for domestic light manufacturing firms in Vietnam in recent years:

- More rapid economic growth has expanded the size of the domestic market.
- Regional integration within the Association of Southeast Asian Nations is increasing the attractiveness of the growing domestic market of Vietnam.
- For Vietnamese firms, the market for competitive light manufacturing is the world. The Trans-Pacific Partnership (TPP), which involves Australia, Brunei Darussalam, Canada, Chile, Japan, Malaysia, Mexico, New Zealand, Peru, Singapore, the United States, and Vietnam as either actively negotiating or signatory countries, represents endless opportunities for Vietnam. The countries potentially involved in the partnership represent more than half of global output and over 40 percent of world trade.[1]

Vietnam has so much potential in light manufacturing because of the comparative advantage of its young labor force and its natural resources. The natural resources are well suited for an expansion of manufacturing capacity that can replace imports and capture overseas markets for processed agricultural products, wood, leather goods, and garments. Vietnam's greatest asset, however, is its large pool of workers, whose productivity in well-managed firms in some sectors is comparable with the levels observed in China (table 3.1). The labor productivity in the average firm is low, but, with the aid of good management and technical assistance, it can be elevated to the productivity of the most well managed firms without requiring costly training among all workers. The detailed studies undertaken through our project demonstrate the feasibility of achieving substantial management upgrades in small firms through inexpensive, short-term training programs. Furthermore, once begun, the process of upgrading can become self-sustaining, as word spreads of the tangible benefits accruing to early participants in training programs. The chief ingredient is new or improved enterprise management, together with targeted technical assistance, the impact of

Table 3.1 Labor Productivity in Light Manufacturing, China, Ethiopia, and Vietnam, 2010

Product	China	Ethiopia	Vietnam
Polo shirts, pieces per employee per day	18–35	7–19	8–14
Leather loafers, pieces per employee per day	3–7	1–7	1–6
Wooden chairs, pieces per employee per day	3–6	0.2–0.4	1–3
Crown corks (bottle caps), 1,000 pieces per employee per day	13–25	10	25–27
Wheat processing, tons per employee per day	0.2–0.4	0.6–1.9	0.6–0.8

Source: GDS 2011.

which has been shown in other countries.[2] Attracting new investors, particularly overseas entrepreneurs who can provide hands-on production and marketing experience in target industries, as well as financial resources and technical expertise, can accelerate industrial expansion and structural change.

Up to now, Vietnam's industrialization strategy has relied on the assembly of final products, mainly from imported inputs. To raise the value added of its goods, Vietnam needs to integrate the large informal domestic enterprises into the economy and global trade and also integrate the supply chain of the assembly activities of large formal firms into the economy by investing in the upstream production of the goods in which it has a comparative advantage in production and in which it has already established a market share, such as agribusiness, garments, and wood.[3] Unlike downstream activities, however, the production of the associated raw materials and intermediate goods is capital intensive and technology driven, and it requires skilled labor. Inviting foreign direct investment (FDI) into these areas and reforming education and vocational systems are the best means to reach this goal. For this reason, the government should undertake a complete review of the incentives for FDI so as to focus on upstream production and on bringing in capital and technical expertise, while improving labor and entrepreneurial skills. More efficient organization can yield huge savings in transport costs in industries that are far from ports and require land transport of high-volume, heavy materials. The commercialization of domestic inputs, such as timber, bamboo, and leather, can save time, as well as foreign exchange, and can increase the capacity of domestic producers to respond quickly to shifts in demand.

A Key Roadblock: The Missing Middle

In light manufacturing in particular, a prerequisite for exporting is the ability to fill large orders in price- and quality-competitive products in a short time. This requires tapping into scale economies associated with labor-intensive, assembly line production chains, that is, large firm operations. By definition, smaller firms cannot do this.

The striking paucity of medium and large firms explains why, in general, Vietnam's domestic firms do not participate in international trade and why economic growth has thus far led to a widening trade deficit (see chapter 2).

Because the population of light industry enterprises is skewed toward small firms, light manufacturing is constrained from playing a greater role in the domestic economy and virtually debarred from the export sector.

One explanation for the near absence of large domestic firms in light manufacturing in Vietnam revolves around the skills required to organize and manage medium and large firms. Sutton and Kellow (2010) point out that, in Ethiopia, the capabilities of small entrepreneurs are not adequate for graduating to medium manufacturers, who need in-depth industry knowledge and experience in managing a certain scale of operation. Söderbom (2011, 7) finds that, in Ethiopia, "a worker in a firm with 50 or more employees produces as much value added in just over an hour as does a worker in a microenterprise in a (10-hour) day."

Another explanation may be that, unlike the Vietnamese government, other Asian governments facilitate the process whereby small enterprises grow into medium and large firms (see the policy section on direct and indirect exporters below). Firm size in poor countries is positively associated with the stock of capital, machinery, and land, though information on land is sparse (Fafchamps and Quinn 2012). This association may explain why firms in China's industrial parks can overcome hurdles and gain access to these factors, exploit scale economies through modern technology that facilitates assembly line production, and grow into larger firms.

Our qualitative firm interviews validate this hypothesis. The vast majority of informal firm owners in Vietnam do not have access to land to expand the scale of production. So, while they do not need finance to start up, they cannot easily grow to the size of other East Asian firms. The lack of land ownership precludes, of course, the use of land as collateral to obtain financing to purchase more advanced machinery and increase productivity. Clearly, government attention to the land issue among informal firms is crucial to any efforts to jump-start light manufacturing in Vietnam.

A large number of small domestic firms in Vietnam engage in low-productivity work. The vast majority of firms are small, and many are owned and operated by households, mostly in the informal sector. Currently, about 35 percent of urban workers are active in the informal sector. In many countries in the region, wages in the informal sector are far lower than wages in the formal sector. The implications of this gap are clear. Low wages in Vietnam are a signal of the low productivity of the labor force employed in agriculture and in the urban informal sector.

The presence of so many state-owned enterprises (SOEs) in manufacturing is another major reason small private enterprises in Vietnam cannot grow (chapter 2). In China, virtually all SOEs in light manufacturing have been privatized. In addition to privatizing SOEs, the Vietnamese government should aim at fostering competition among the remaining enterprises. Overwhelming evidence from new research, including our research, indicates that the constraints on firms vary by firm size; so, a one-size-fits-all approach is unlikely to be effective. Small and large firms need to be treated differently, with the eventual goal of integrating them into comprehensive value chains.

Policy Interventions

Would policy interventions help address this dual industrial structure? As explained in one of our previous volumes, the priorities and sequencing of policy interventions should follow four criteria (see Dinh and others 2012). First, policy interventions should be undertaken only if a market failure—existence of a pure public good, externalities, noncompetitive markets resulting from policy distortions, information asymmetries, or coordination problems—prevents the private market from adequately playing its role. Second, these interventions should focus on sectors and subsectors that demonstrate the most potential for comparative advantage and job growth. Third, they should be cost effective in the short and long runs, with limited fiscal impact. Fourth, implementation capacity and the implications for governance and the political economy of the reforms should be thoroughly assessed.

The weak links between domestic small and medium enterprises (SMEs) and foreign-invested enterprises in Vietnam reflect the high costs of transactions among manufacturing firms, as well as between firms and traders. These transaction costs arise because of asymmetric information and imperfect contract enforcement and result in adverse selection and delays; underinvestment in public goods such as roads, electricity, and communications; and imperfect credit markets.[4]

Historically, the East Asian economies (including China; Japan; the Republic of Korea; Singapore, and Taiwan, China) have relied on a number of policy instruments to promote industrial development: equal treatment for direct and indirect exporters, the establishment of trading companies as a means to increase exports and reduce transaction costs, the use of industrial parks and industrial clusters (cluster-based industrial development) to reduce transaction costs and enhance competitiveness, and the introduction of the Kaizen method to improve management knowledge and lower production costs. These policies are not exhaustive and can be combined.

Equal Treatment for Direct and Indirect Exporters

Historically, East Asian economies (including Japan, Korea, Singapore, and Taiwan, China) integrated domestic producers with formal exporters by providing the same incentives for direct exporters and indirect exporters. Rhee (1985) provides an excellent detailed discussion of these policies. He distinguishes two types of indirect exporters: (1) indirect exporters who supply intermediate inputs to final stage (or next stage) export manufacturers and (2) indirect exporters who supply finished export products to trading companies that export directly (or sell to other trading companies). Indirect exporters are usually manufacturers, but they can also be pure traders. The policy instruments used to equalize incentives include (1) flexible and realistic exchange rates, (2) free trade in inputs and outputs, (3) competitive financial and money markets, (4) competitive primary input markets, and (5) nondiscriminatory domestic taxes. For example, earlier in its industrialization process, Korea exempted import duties and taxes on intermediate inputs among all exporters, direct or indirect and inside or outside the free trade zones and bonded manufacturing warehouses. To achieve this goal while still maintaining an import protection system on the rest of the economy, it used a set of input coefficients to calculate the needed imports of intermediate inputs. When this is combined with automatic import licensing and free access to foreign exchange among both direct and indirect exporters, industrial producers creating export value added are able to choose freely between imported and domestic inputs (at world market prices), irrespective of whether their production occurs at the final stage or some earlier stage.

Given their imperfect financial and capital markets during the earlier stages of industrialization, the East Asian economies also provided guaranteed automatic access to financing at the same interest rates for all export activities among both direct and indirect exporters. In Korea, the financing for indirect exporters was accomplished through the domestic letter of credit system (Rhee 1985). In this system, when an exporter has an export letter of credit, this induces his/her bank to open a second, similar credit account on behalf of the exporter, with the input-supplying indirect exporter or output-supplying indirect exporter as the beneficiary. "Thus, the indirect exporter gains access to all export incentives based on the receipt of the domestic L/C [letter of credit], just as the final exporter gains such access based on the receipt of an export L/C (or other evidence of an export order)" Rhee (1985, 112–13). Another policy used by Korea to encourage indirect exporters was to provide preshipment working capital loans (usually for less than 90 days) designed to meet the financing needs for production or sales activities. Postshipment finance (granted for up to 180 days) was also available, covering the financing needs between shipment time and payment.

Encouraging the Establishment and Expansion of Trading Companies[5]

The concept of trading companies used in this report is not equivalent to the term as commonly known and used in Vietnam. The term in Vietnam refers to companies, mostly SOEs, that were once allocated foreign exchange for imports or exports. Our concept denotes private enterprises that facilitate international trade and industrialization through several channels, including the achievement of economies of scale and scope in overseas distribution by subcontracting and leveraging knowledge about foreign markets and export processes across multiple client firms and products; reducing transaction, search, negotiation, and information costs; introducing new trends and machinery, resulting in the manufacture of products that are competitive in international markets; providing access to finance; organizing production lines; and undertaking quality control. In Japan, examples are companies such as Mitsubishi and Sumitomo.

Historically, such intermediaries have played a major, often unrecognized role in facilitating trade. The long list of countries that have relied on trading companies to improve trade deficits includes Japan; Korea; Taiwan, China; Thailand; Turkey; and even the United States.[6] The rationale for using trading companies varies. Companies may choose to export directly or indirectly based on productivity. Productive firms that can afford to establish their own distribution networks export directly; less productive firms may export indirectly through intermediaries, while the least productive firms target the domestic market. Ahn, Khandelwal, and Wei (2011) provide a theoretical model for the role of intermediaries in facilitating trade.[7] Using firm-level data in China to supply empirical evidence for their predictions, they show that Chinese firms that export indirectly are more likely to export directly later on. These predictions are in line with the business literature on trading companies that has relied on transaction cost theory to analyze these issues.[8]

The benefits of trading firms vary with the products traded and the volume of the trade (Roehl 1983, cited in Jones 2000). For some standardized products and bulk commodities, the use of export intermediation might be more beneficial than internalization because trading companies can reduce the transaction costs of both buyers and sellers. However, firms are more likely to choose direct trade if the volume of trade is high, supply and demand are stable, specification is more complex, and quality assurance is difficult (Jones 2000). Also, Ahn, Khandelwal, and Wei (2011) find that intermediary firms in China focus more on particular countries, while direct exporters tend to focus on particular products. This lends support to the view that intermediaries are a means to overcome the market-specific costs related to international trade. Trading companies would strengthen the links in Vietnam between domestic companies and export markets, including foreign-invested enterprises.

The Chinese government has helped create markets for trading intermediaries by lifting the restrictions imposed because of state monopolies; by liberalizing access to trade, thereby establishing the environment necessary for fair competition and allowing trading companies to take full responsibility for their profits and losses; and by promoting export-oriented policies. At the local and provincial levels, officials of industrial zones have recognized the vital importance of trading companies in matchmaking and have provided incentives to promote them.

Trading companies offer a plethora of benefits for the local economy. They are a great source of revenue for industrial zones. They contribute to tax revenue and, by serving manufacturers in the zones, especially SMEs, help develop manufacturing, which also increases tax revenue.

As in Japan, Korea, and other East Asian countries, China's experience shows that trading intermediaries are important not only in facilitating trade, but also in overcoming the major constraints that manufacturers face in the initial stages of industrialization. These constraints include problems in the access to cost and quality of inputs; in the access to industrial land; in the access to financing; and in trade logistics, entrepreneurial skills, and worker skills (Dinh and others 2013).

Trading companies help smaller and larger manufacturers to explore new markets and enhance their competitiveness through constant product and technology upgrades. They propose options—including facilitating independent export or import by manufacturers, along with guidance in successfully negotiating the fierce competition in many dimensions—that support light manufacturing ventures ranging from small start-ups to large, sophisticated producers in many industries. The collaboration of producers with trading companies has yielded many advantages, such as lower transaction costs, the availability of more market information, and financial benefits. Trading companies can help small enterprises integrate with larger companies and gain access to foreign markets, expertise, technology, and ideas. Chinese manufacturers have profited from these services and increased their exports dramatically over the past 20 years. Such growth would not have been possible without the liberalization of foreign trade and the contributions of trading companies.

Trading companies have made important contributions to China's economic success. These companies perform a crucial function by matching importers with local manufacturers, facilitating communication among firms, and assisting in the shipment of goods from suppliers to buyers. Operating at a critical juncture of the market, the companies have become vital go-betweens in the booming world of processing trade. Maintaining a network of suppliers, they help firms find missing markets and provide diverse domestic firms with enhanced access to imports of materials and components. They also assist firms in controlling costs and enhancing quality and variety. Moreover, their relationship with intermediaries forces domestic producers to improve to compete effectively with imports.

Foreign traders in China began as domestic firms in processing trade under favorable terms. These activities represented a major pathway for firms to become involved in international trade. As time passed, the firms evolved into trading companies as the incentives for companies and governments changed. This led to better performance among trading companies, particularly after the Chinese government ended state monopolies through a series of gradual reforms and allowed private companies to conduct foreign trade. Pilot reforms were first implemented in special zones and then extended to coastal regions and, finally, throughout the country. The end of the state monopoly on trading companies facilitated the entry of private producers and traders. As reforms continued, China eliminated mandatory export targets and import plans, allowing market forces to determine production. Tariff reductions also boosted processed exports.

In China today, firms specializing in trade are heterogeneous. Three main types of firms provide intermediary trade services in China: foreign trade companies (also referred to as trading companies), service providers (service-specific agencies), and the offices of representatives. Most of the trading companies and agencies are private or foreign owned (often subsidiaries of trading companies in Hong Kong SAR, China, or in Taiwan, China), while state-owned trading companies are responsible for trade in regulated commodities, such as steel, acrylic acid, and timber. Figure 3.1 depicts how local manufacturers link with foreign buyers and describes the services provided by trading companies.

Foreign Trade Companies

In China, foreign trade companies are involved exclusively in trade. They are divided into two types based on mode of operation: the buy-and-sell model and the agency model. The first type includes conventional trading firms that

Figure 3.1 How Foreign Buyers and Local Manufacturers Connect, China

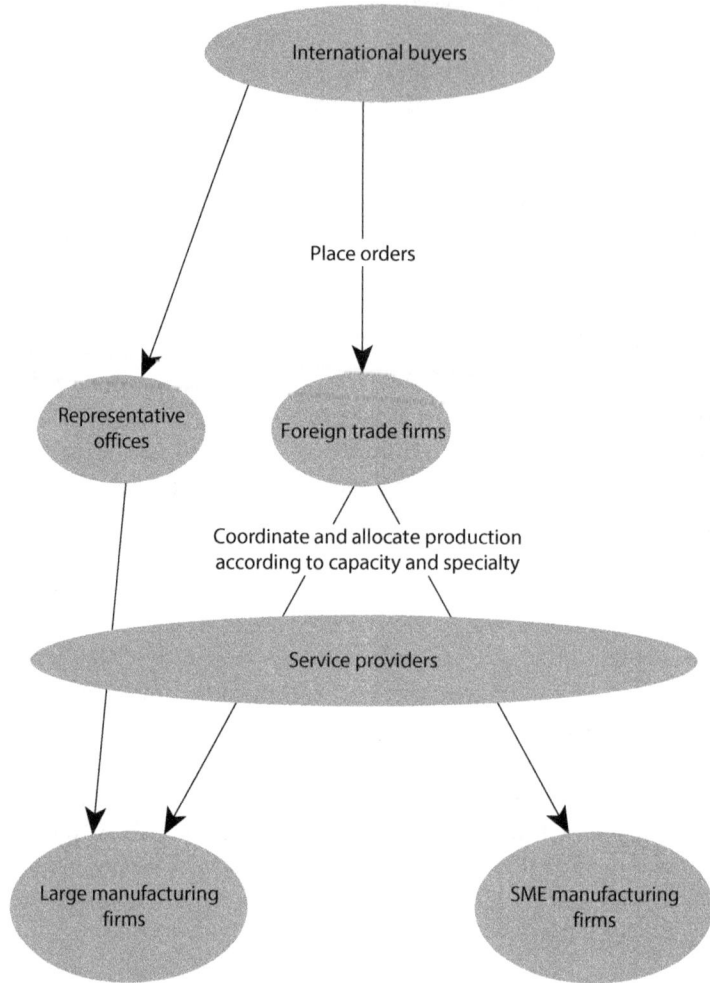

Source: Dinh and others 2013.

purchase commodities from input suppliers or manufacturers, sell them to manufacturers or groups of overseas buyers, and profit from the difference in the purchase price and the selling price (the buyout operational model). The second type includes trading companies that earn commissions by providing information on market demand for manufacturing companies, assist in negotiations between suppliers and buyers, and supervise the delivery of goods. The commission ranges from 0.8 to 3.0 percent of the market value of the goods.[9] This process does not require a large amount of capital and is therefore the major business model for small and medium trading firms.

Trading firms provide three core functions that facilitate trade and have helped China become an export powerhouse. First, trading firms usually maintain a network of manufacturers and subcontract orders based on the capacity and technology of these manufacturers. If required, they search for new production units and help the units already in their networks expand production. Second, trading firms identify potential foreign buyers for the products of their manufacturing clients. They then connect the two parties and help with the negotiations and the development of the products. Third, in some cases, to cope with rapidly growing markets and globalization, trading companies expand their services to include production chain services—along the lines of the well-known model of Everich in Shenzhen, Guangdong Province, and Li & Fung in Hong Kong SAR, China—and production and management consultancy to reduce production costs and enhance manufacturer competitiveness.

Service Providers

Service providers (service-specific agencies) offer services to manufacturing companies that help ease customs clearance procedures, payment collection, and foreign exchange settlements. These service providers are often exporters themselves, making extra profits by taking advantage of their access to export certificates and foreign exchange accounts. They do not provide the comprehensive services of foreign trade companies; rather, the suppliers and the buyers establish their own contacts (directly or through a foreign trade firm) and then hire the agency to furnish the logistics.

Representative Offices

Many large overseas buyers have set up subsidiaries in China to produce goods for their parent companies and for other clients. Such offices offer services similar to those of foreign trade companies, but focus on the interests of their parent companies. They identify manufacturers and distribute orders according to the needs of their parent companies and the capacity and specialty of the manufacturers.

Industrial Parks: Vehicles to Integrate Domestic SMEs into the Economy

While providing important short-term investment, employment, and foreign exchange benefits, as in China, industrial parks could also help Vietnam in the pursuit of strategic long-run objectives, including technology and skill transfers, the multiplier effects on regional development, and the expansion of upstream and downstream industrial links. Industrial parks offer the quickest route to profits and technology acquisition in an environment in which sweeping economy-wide reforms are not feasible because of either financial constraints or political issues (the persistence of contrary ideologies or the entrenched interests of officials and bureaucracies associated with the plan system).

Until now, the purpose of industrial parks in Vietnam has been to encourage FDI rather than to help promote domestic manufacturing firms to grow. In contrast, in China, the system of plug-and-play industrial parks oriented toward SMEs plays a key role in encouraging the development of domestic light manufacturing (Dinh and others 2013). This policy tool has been used extensively in East Asia and has helped simultaneously resolve the main binding constraints in light manufacturing: the lack of access to industrial land; the shortage of input industries; and deficiencies in finance, trade logistics, worker skills, managerial skills, and infrastructure. The parks have enabled many Chinese SMEs to grow from family operations focused on domestic markets into global powerhouses.

Successful industrial parks in China provide enterprises with security, good basic infrastructure (roads, energy, water, sewerage), streamlined government regulations (through government service centers), and affordable industrial land. They also offer technical training, low-cost standardized factory shells that allow entrepreneurs to plug and play, and free and decent worker housing next to plants. By helping small enterprises grow into medium and large enterprises, China has avoided the shortage of medium firms—the missing middle—faced by most developing countries. More advanced industrial parks offer services in market analysis, accounting, import and export information, and management advice and help firms recruit and train workers. For example, parks in or near the Yangzi River Delta place a strong emphasis on assisting firms in obtaining business licenses and in hiring workers. Parks may also include facilities to address environmental challenges.

Plug-and-play industrial parks have greatly reduced the start-up costs and risks among SMEs that have sufficient scale, capital, and growth prospects to take advantage of larger facilities during a phase in their development when they are unable to acquire bank loans. They have also facilitated industrial clusters, generating substantial spillovers and economies of scale and scope among Chinese industries. The clusters likewise benefit from the government support for input and output markets. China's parks focus on specific industries, such as leather and textiles in Nanchang, furniture in Ji'an, and electronics in Ganzhou (Sonobe, Hu, and Otsuka 2002; Sonobe and Otsuka 2006; Zeng 2010).

Industrial parks could help Vietnam circumvent several constraints on the development and competitiveness of domestic firms, including the shortages in inputs, industrial land, finance, trade logistics, and entrepreneurial and worker skills.

Input Industries

If domestic input markets are underdeveloped and inputs must be imported, import tariffs raise costs. Yet, the removal of the tariffs on all the inputs used in domestic production, while improving the global competiveness of local producers, could have an adverse impact on government revenue and could face opposition from incumbent suppliers. China has used industrial parks to avoid these disadvantages by limiting any allowed tariff exemptions to inputs that are imported, processed, and then reexported as part of the final output produced within the parks. China has also sought to accelerate technology transfers by allowing duty-free imports of industrial machinery for export-oriented firms in special zones and industrial parks.

Industrial Land

Manufacturing requires access to affordable land. In China in the early 1980s, industrial land with efficient infrastructure was in short supply even in the more well developed coastal regions. To circumvent this constraint, local officials provided fully serviced land in industrial parks, sometimes with plug-and-play factory shells that allowed entrepreneurs to commence production without having to build factories. Eventually, local governments facilitated access to industrial land throughout the domestic economy. Government entities gradually developed policies that enabled smaller firms to expand organically or through industrial parks that eased the constraints in land and infrastructure.

In general, the expansion of industrialization and urbanization reduce the land available for production and commerce. Relocating enterprises to industrial parks or economic development zones is a major channel for supplying new land for manufacturing. Industrial parks, normally developed by local governments, offer roads, utility connections, and standardized workshops. By convincing firms to move into industrial parks, local governments also hope to group firms in the same sector so as to reap the benefits of agglomeration and clustering (see below).

Finance

In China as well as in Vietnam, state-owned banks lend largely to borrowers with strong ties to the public sector and discriminate against small privately owned firms of the type found in light manufacturing clusters. By moving these small firms to industrial parks, local governments can allow them to use land as collateral to obtain funds for developing light manufacturing. In China, local officials have also used their networks and influence to assist firms in gaining access to external finance.

Improving Trade Facilitation and Logistics

By locating industrial parks in coastal areas with access to domestic transport and port facilities and with long histories of international trade, exporters in Vietnam could enjoy enhanced trade logistics. As the volume of manufactured exports expands, investments in export-related transport and port facilities become more attractive. Industrial park administrations could also streamline the customs formalities faced by entrepreneurs.

At the moment, there is a missing link between infrastructure planning and trade in Vietnam, as indicated in a recent World Bank report (Pham and others 2013). SMEs in Vietnam would greatly benefit from government policies to facilitate trade and logistics in three areas: transport infrastructure and logistics services, regulatory procedures for exports and imports, and supply chains. The successful implementation of the policies recommended in the Bank report would go a long way toward helping industrial parks and clusters and the manufacturing sector grow.

Entrepreneurial and Worker Skills

Industrial parks provide permanent space for overseas and local investors, thus attracting entrepreneurs with the managerial and technical skills needed to run successful businesses. As local industries grow, so do the local pool of experienced workers and the availability of ancillary services and goods, including domestic supplies of material inputs. These developments reinforce one another and raise the productivity of local industry.

Encouraging Organic Clusters through Industrial Parks and Other Policies

Another way to help SMEs grow (rather than merely establishing them, the focus of Vietnamese government policy) is to encourage clusters. An industrial cluster usually currently features a group of enterprises and institutions that share a specific kind of business activity in a limited geographical area. Industrial clusters are common in developing countries among SMEs producing similar or related products. Examples include shoe, garment, furniture, woodworking, and metalwork clusters. In Vietnam, the tradition of clusters has existed for thousands of years, but the growth of clusters has never been subject to any policy of explicit promotion, as it is in China and other countries.

The advantages of clusters are many. Clustering contributes to industrial development by mitigating market failures, including the lack of markets and technology information, information asymmetry, moral hazard, and imperfect contract enforcement (Sonobe, Suzuki, and Otsuka 2011). Because of their geographic proximity, firms can trade intermediate goods and services with other firms in the cluster more easily, resulting in lower transaction and monitoring costs. Moreover, information and technology exchange is facilitated so that enterprises can learn from each other (information spillovers). Clusters foster the emergence of labor markets for specialized skills, making it easier to find workers with desired skills. Clusters can likewise help attract customers, suppliers, and traders.

The advantages of clustering are more apparent among SMEs than among larger companies because it is more difficult and costly for SMEs to (1) absorb new technologies, materials, and ideas in production, management, and marketing; (2) test new practices; (3) integrate production processes; (4) find good transacting partners (suppliers, traders, and so on); (5) monitor parts and materials suppliers; (6) find good, well-skilled workers; (7) find customers; (8) ensure the collection of payments; and (9) punish betrayers or cheaters (Sonobe 2007).

Empirical studies have shown that industries participating in a successful cluster register higher employment and wage growth and more manufacturing establishments and patents. Healthy cluster environments are often also associated with more new industries. Once a few firms in an industry form a cluster in a local community, the entry costs for other firms become lower because of positive external economies (Fujita, Krugman, and Mori 1999). The development of effective transfers of information and technology within clusters creates opportunities for the emergence of other industries and clusters.

A cluster strategy can help overcome typical constraints on business development and growth in low-income economies (inputs, industrial land, finance, trade logistics, entrepreneurial skills, and worker skills). The solutions offered by a cluster strategy are unique to each country. Firms in clusters may grow in different ways to break free of the constraints. One example is worker skills. In a cluster, as people engage with one another, knowledge is quickly diffused through the local community. A worker who encounters technical difficulties can often find the solution by discussing the difficulties with others in the cluster. Workers can also move to other firms in the cluster within the same industry, expanding their professional learning. Besides such incidental learning opportunities in clusters, local government can build formal vocational schools or collaborate with universities to provide training programs targeting specific industries.

Cluster growth and upgrading have been largely an outcome of market mechanisms because entrepreneurs in clusters have creatively mobilized knowledge, resources, and capital in and outside local communities based on comparative advantage. However, the creation of industrial clusters in developing countries with a small knowledge pool, inadequate infrastructure, and limited technological expertise and labor skills has required active government involvement.

In China, various levels of government—local, provincial, and central—have worked together to form and implement cluster policies. Local governments in China have been particularly supportive of clusters (Dinh and others 2013). Because of the direct connection to communities, local officials offer services to promote entrepreneurial activity. Such measures to foster cluster development include nurturing clusters from an existing industrial base, building industrial parks, creating special platforms for specific industries, and tailoring policies to the business life cycle of firms and clusters.

Unlike the Chinese central government's 1980s strategy of building national champions, cluster-based industrialization in today's China emphasizes locally grown entrepreneurship. Entrepreneurs, rather than governments, establish clusters. At the initial stages of cluster formation, when production is concentrated in home workshops, little intervention by the government occurs on the concept that the wrong kind of intervention can snuff out promising advances. Once clusters begin to expand, the public sector can undertake a more active involvement to develop general infrastructure (roads, utilities, land) and facilities that meet the specific requirements of the emerging clusters (market structures, financial institutions, training programs, quality control mechanisms, and so on).

China's experience has made clear that government should nurture clusters—not try to create them—by identifying and applying incentive-compatible industrial policies. During the quality improvement phase, the government could provide credit through low interest loans. The optimal approach would consist of offering credit only to firms with a record of successful innovation. The government might also offer favorable income tax treatment, a policy that has been used successfully in China. Finally, it should aim at strengthening subcontracting. Incentives should be provided to encourage subcontracting links (and competition) between small and large firms as part of industrial value chains and clusters. In China, such links, along with competitive dynamics, are key in the low-cost operations and in the flexibility of manufacturers in filling a great variety of customer orders. Small firms obtain work orders through subcontracts with larger firms that, in turn, rely on the smaller firms and their specialized skills to keep production costs down.

Kaizen Programs[10]

Management is considered a major determinant of productivity and has been identified as a significant factor in multifaceted innovation (Sonobe and Otsuka 2011; Syverson 2011). Our study indicates that Kaizen management—a commonsense, low-cost management method that seeks to enhance quality, cost, and delivery by gradually improving work processes—can be helpful to SMEs. Moreover, unlike European management, Japanese management focuses on the active involvement of all staff categories in identifying and implementing ongoing improvements. The five steps in the framework of Kaizen are teamwork, personal discipline, improved morale, quality circles, and suggestions for improvement.

In many SMEs in developing countries, production processes result in poor quality, low cost, poor delivery, and significant variability. A good starting point for applying the Kaizen method is the reduction of inefficiency and variability through the application of the first three steps of the five-step framework. Firms could begin by sorting the equipment (machinery, tools, jigs, dies, works in progress, raw materials, and old versions of documents) and removing unnecessary items from the workplace. This ensures a more rapid and safer production process because it helps eliminate the time wasted looking for tools and materials that are not at hand and the work stoppages occurring because materials are not ready. Better maintenance of machinery and tools would minimize machine breakdowns. It is estimated that more than 70 percent of machine breakdowns can be prevented simply by timely oiling, dusting, and the tightening of nuts and bolts. The advantages of the Kaizen method have been recognized by SMEs in Africa and Asia according to field activities carried out by our project team, which conducted two Kaizen experiments during the work on four case studies: a metalwork cluster in Ethiopia, a garment cluster in Tanzania, and a knitwear cluster and a steel cluster in Vietnam.

Conclusion

Policy measures to improve the competitiveness of Vietnam must address both the problems of the numerous small, informal, mostly household firms producing for the domestic market and the problems faced by a relatively small number of large, foreign-invested enterprises producing for export. Among small firms, the main issue is to discover ways to nurture growth into larger firms that can achieve greater productivity. This will require improvements in labor skills and technology and in the number, quality, and variety of the products able to compete with imports. Policies to reduce the role of SOEs, provide equal treatment

for direct and indirect exporters, promote trading companies, encourage clustering and subcontracting, attract FDI to upstream activities, use industrial zones
to integrate supply chains, and promote Kaizen training are important in this
respect.

Among larger formal enterprises, the main issue is to find ways to move up
the value addition of the goods produced by increasing the variety and quality
of production. Trade facilitation and logistics are critical for these enterprises.
(These issues are addressed elsewhere; see Pham and others 2013.) The transformation of skills, the transfer of technology, and the building of managerial capacity that are now most effective in foreign-invested enterprises should be applied
to domestic enterprises. From a foreign producer's standpoint, it does not matter
whether the raw materials and intermediate goods are procured in Vietnam or
somewhere else, as long as they are of good quality and price competitive and
can be delivered quickly. It is therefore entirely up to Vietnamese policy makers
and the private sector to make this transformation possible.

So far, Vietnam's economic growth has been based on low-cost, low-skilled
labor, combined with capital from abroad. Together with rising agricultural
output because of the improvement in agricultural productivity, this model has
succeeded in creating a large number of jobs in labor-intensive sectors geared
toward producing exportable goods. However, as Vietnam advances to a higher
per capita income category, this model needs to be modified to help domestic
producers achieve more value added.

Chapters 4–8 examine the constraints on this advance for both types of enterprises (small informal firms as well as large formal firms) and propose solutions
in each of the sectors under study.[11] The final chapter synthesizes the results
across these sectors and discusses how a reform program could be implemented.

Notes

1. See "Trans-Pacific Partnership: Frequently Asked Questions," Office of the United
   States Trade Representative, Washington, DC, http://www.ustr.gov/sites/default/files
   /TPPFAQ.pdf.

2. For example, the Ramsay Shoe Factory was able to export to Italy thanks to the
   foreign technical assistance provided to Ethiopian shoe manufacturers. See Dinh and
   others (2012).

3. This does not apply to agriculture or reprocessing activities.

4. For example, see Akerlof (1970), Hart and Moore (1990), Williamson (1985).

5. This subsection on trading companies has been prepared by Eleonora Mavroeidi.

6. See Cho (1987) for a survey.

7. Ahn, Khandelwal, and Wei (2011) extend the model of heterogeneous firms proposed
   by Melitz (2003) to include firms that can export directly to foreign markets by
   incurring the fixed export and trade costs, while adding an intermediation component.
   In this case, companies can export indirectly through an intermediary firm by incurring "a one-time global fixed cost that provides indirect access to all markets, which
   allows firms to save on market-specific bilateral fixed costs." The model predicts that

the "share of exports through intermediaries is larger in countries with smaller market size, higher variable trade costs, or higher fixed costs of exporting" (Ahn, Khandelwal, and Wei 2011, 73–76).

8. This theory suggests that "the market is costly and inefficient for undertaking certain transactions, and for that reason firms internalize activities in order to minimize transactions costs" (Jones 2000, 4). Transaction cost theory focuses on the actual costs incurred in the process of economic exchange, which most likely result from "the bounded rationality of decision makers, [the] uncertainty and complexity of the environment, and [the] asymmetric distribution of information between parties to an exchange" (Peng and York 2001, 329). Within this framework, "economic agents select those contractual mechanisms that minimize the sum of production costs and the costs of contracting" (Levy 1991, 162).

9. Based on interviews among Chinese manufacturers by our team in 2012.

10. This subsection is based on Sonobe, Suzuki, and Otsuka (2011). See also World Bank (2011).

11. The analysis presented in chapters 4–8 is based on our consultant report, GDS (2011).

References

Ahn, JaeBin, Amit K. Khandelwal, and Shang-Jin Wei. 2011. "The Role of Intermediaries in Facilitating Trade." *Journal of International Economics* 84 (1): 73–85.

Akerlof, George A. 1970. "The Market for 'Lemons': Quality Uncertainty and the Market Mechanism." *Quarterly Journal of Economics* 84 (3): 488–500.

Cho, Dong-Sung. 1987. *The General Trading Company: Concept and Strategy*. Lanham, MD: Lexington Books.

Dinh, Hinh T., Vincent Palmade, Vandana Chandra, and France Cossar. 2012. *Light Manufacturing in Africa: Targeted Policies to Enhance Private Investment and Create Jobs*. Washington, DC: World Bank. http://go.worldbank.org/ASG0J44350.

Dinh, Hinh T., Thomas G. Rawski, Ali Zafar, Lihong Wang, and Eleonora Mavroeidi. 2013. *Tales from the Development Frontier: How China and Other Countries Harness Light Manufacturing to Create Jobs and Prosperity*. With Xin Tong and Pengfei Li. Washington, DC: World Bank.

Fafchamps, Marcel, and Simon Quinn. 2012. "Results of Sample Surveys of Firms." In *Performance of Manufacturing Firms in Africa: An Empirical Analysis*, edited by Hinh T. Dinh and George R. G. Clarke, 139–211. Washington, DC: World Bank.

Fujita, Masahisa, Paul Krugman, and Tomoya Mori. 1999. "On the Evolution of Hierarchical Urban Systems." *European Economic Review* 43 (2): 209–51.

GDS (Global Development Solutions). 2011. *The Value Chain and Feasibility Analysis; Domestic Resource Cost Analysis*. Vol. 2 of *Light Manufacturing in Africa: Targeted Policies to Enhance Private Investment and Create Jobs*. Washington, DC: World Bank. http://go.worldbank.org/6G2A3TFI20.

Hart, Olivier, and John Moore. 1990. "Property Rights and the Nature of the Firm." *Journal of Political Economy* 98 (6): 1119–58.

Jones, Geoffrey. 2000. *Merchants to Multinationals: British Trading Companies in the Nineteenth and Twentieth Centuries*. New York: Oxford University Press.

Levy, Brian. 1991. "Transactions Costs, the Size of Firms, and Industrial Policy: Lessons from a Comparative Case Study of the Footwear Industry in Korea and Taiwan." *Journal of Development Economics* 34 (1–2): 151–78.

Melitz, Marc J. 2003. "The Impact of Trade on Intra-Industry Reallocations and Aggregate Industry Productivity." *Econometrica* 71 (6): 1695–725.

Peng, Mike W., and Anne S. York. 2001. "Behind Intermediary Performance in Export Trade: Transactions, Agents, and Resources." *Journal of International Business Studies* 32 (2): 327–46.

Pham, Duc Minh, Deepak Mishra, Kee-Cheok Cheong, John Arnold, Anh Minh Trinh, Huyen Thi Ngoc Ngo, and Hien Thi Phuong Nguyen. 2013. *Trade Facilitation, Value Creation, and Competitiveness: Policy Implications for Vietnam's Economic Growth.* Vol. 1. Hanoi: World Bank.

Rhee, Yung Whee. 1985. *Instruments for Export Policy and Administration: Lessons from the East Asian Experience.* World Bank Staff Working Paper 725, World Bank, Washington, DC.

Roehl, Thomas. 1983. "A Transactions Cost Approach to International Trading Structures: The Case of the Japanese General Trading Companies." *Hitotsubashi Journal of Economics* 24 (2): 119–35.

Söderbom, Måns. 2011. "Firm Size and Structural Change: A Case Study of Ethiopia." Paper presented at the African Economic Research Consortium's Biannual Research Workshop, Nairobi, May 29. http://www.soderbom.net/plenary_final.pdf.

Sonobe, Tetsushi. 2007. "The Advantage of Industrial Cluster for the SME Development." Paper presented at the Asian Development Bank Institute's "Industrial Development Planning: Cluster-Based Development Approach Policy Seminar," Tokyo, May 14–19. http://www.adbi.org/conf-seminar-papers/2007/04/04/2210.industrial.clusters.sme .dev/.

Sonobe, Tetsushi, Dinghuan Hu, and Keijiro Otsuka. 2002. "Process of Cluster Formation in China: A Case Study of a Garment Town." *Journal of Development Studies* 39 (1): 118–39.

Sonobe, Tetsushi, and Keijiro Otsuka. 2006. *Cluster-Based Industrial Development: An East Asian Model.* Basingstoke, U.K.: Palgrave Macmillan.

———. 2011. *Cluster-Based Industrial Development: A Comparative Study of Asia and Africa.* Basingstoke, U.K.: Palgrave Macmillan.

Sonobe, Tetsushi, Aya Suzuki, and Keijiro Otsuka. 2011. "Reports on the Immediate Impact of the Classroom Training Program Based on the Baseline Survey and the First Post-Training Survey." In *Kaizen for Managerial Skills Improvement in Small and Medium Enterprises: An Impact Evaluation Study,* 18–277. Vol. 4 of *Light Manufacturing in Africa: Targeted Policies to Enhance Private Investment and Create Jobs.* Washington, DC: World Bank. http://go.worldbank.org/4Y1QF5FIB0.

Sutton, John, and Nebil Kellow. 2010. *An Enterprise Map of Ethiopia.* London: International Growth Center.

Syverson, Chad. 2011. "What Determines Productivity?" *Journal of Economic Literature* 49 (2): 326–65.

Williamson, Oliver E. 1985. *The Economic Institutions of Capitalism.* New York: Free Press.

World Bank. 2011. *Kaizen for Managerial Skills Improvement in Small and Medium Enterprises: An Impact Evaluation Study.* Vol. 4 of *Light Manufacturing in Africa: Targeted*

Policies to Enhance Private Investment and Create Jobs. Washington, DC: World Bank. http://go.worldbank.org/4Y1QF5FIB0.

Zeng, Douglas Zhihua. 2010. "How Do Special Economic Zones and Industrial Clusters Drive China's Rapid Development?" In *Building Engines for Growth and Competitiveness in China: Experience with Special Economic Zones and Industrial Clusters*, edited by Douglas Zhihua Zeng, 1–53. Washington, DC: World Bank.

CHAPTER 4

Apparel

In apparel, the supply chain structure and the production system are somewhat different in Vietnam because many manufacturers are foreign owned or are subcontractors for foreign buyers or foreign consolidators in consuming markets. This means that apparel manufacturers in Vietnam are accustomed merely to assembling products. The most binding constraint is inadequate worker skills and poor labor efficiency. The next most binding constraint is the cost of inputs. Our detailed comparative value chain analysis shows that, if Vietnam can take advantage of the new trade arrangement, the Trans-Pacific Partnership (TPP), the country has the potential to become more globally competitive in apparel. Enhancing worker skills should be a priority. There is likewise a need for long-term investment strategies in design, marketing, and the creation of new styles. The government should also facilitate better access to inputs for local producers and improve trade logistics.

Description of the Sector

Vietnam is one of the world's top apparel producers, exporting $8 billion in goods in 2009. Globally, $360 billion in apparel products were traded that year. Apparel is, by far, the most important traded light manufacturing sector among low-income countries. By 2014, the global apparel retail industry is forecast to have a value of $1.2 trillion. China has emerged as the largest apparel exporter and, in particular, the largest exporter of clothing, exporting apparel worth more than $100 billion in 2009. It accounted for less than 10 percent of the market 20 years ago, but today accounts for a third (figure 4.1). China's success offers a constructive example of how Vietnam might bolster its apparel industry. Moreover, because of the erosion in China's advantage in the cost of labor at the periphery, there is an opportunity for Vietnam to fill a void in the global industry.

In 2010, according to the Vietnam National Textile and Garment Group (Vinatex), the apparel sector employed about 1.2 million workers in more than 3,000 officially registered small, medium, and large enterprises (GDS 2011).

Figure 4.1 Leading Apparel Exporters, Worldwide, 2009

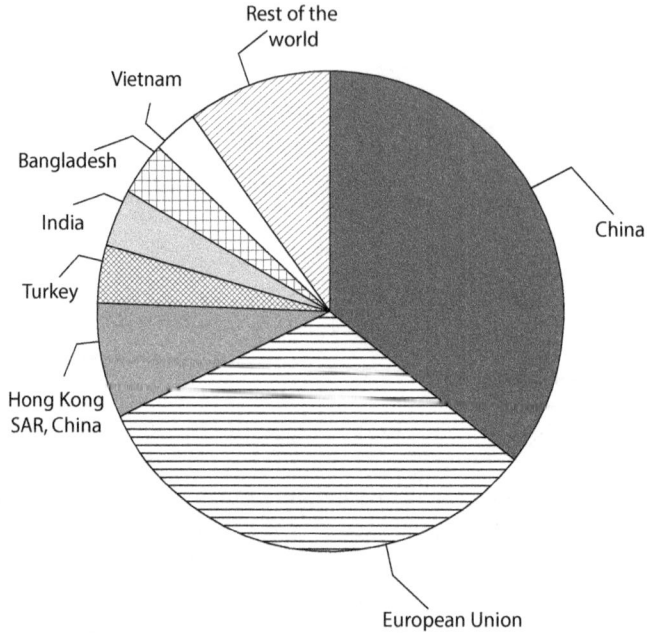

Source: GDS 2011.
Note: Based on World Trade Organization data, which include export processing zone data and differ from the data of UN Comtrade (United Nations Commodity Trade Statistics Database), Statistics Division, Department of Economic and Social Affairs, United Nations, New York, http://comtrade.un.org/db/. The data on China include significant shipments through processing zones. The data on Bangladesh and Vietnam include estimates.

Of these, 18.5 percent were partially or wholly foreign owned (mainly the large companies), and the remainder were non–state-owned and state-owned Vietnamese enterprises.

Although rising labor costs and the recent appreciation of the Chinese yuan have caused many to question China's ability to remain competitive in apparel, China's growing share in global clothing exports illustrates the importance of adjusting to industry trends and of the strength of the value chain, which are both keys to success in the apparel industry. The ability to source large quantities of clothing of consistent quality through an integrated global supply chain from a few suppliers who can deliver the clothing on time is critical among retailers. Thus, a private-label, multiseason fashion retailer in a niche market typically prefers apparel suppliers who exhibit superior performance in order-to-delivery times and who are consistent in quality even if these suppliers charge more. The same holds for large, consolidated retailers. Thus, suppliers in developing countries other than China are often compelled to keep their clothing prices lower because, to be competitive, they must compensate for supply chain deficiencies that render them less desirable. By the same token, for many suppliers, lower prices are generally a necessary, though not sufficient condition for access to the global supply chain of the larger retailers.

Unlike China, the apparel production system and the structure of the supply chain in Vietnam can generally be described as follows:

- The industry preforms mainly cut, make, and trim (CMT) functions on inputs that are provided by buyers or consolidators. There is little free on board (FOB) garment production.[1]
- Because many manufacturers in Vietnam are subcontractors for foreign buyers or foreign consolidators in consuming markets, they have little or no access to or knowledge of input and output supply chain networks in or outside the country.
- Because the buyers or consolidators also provide all the product and engineering specifications, as well as the production equipment, apparel manufacturers in Vietnam have not developed in-house design and engineering capabilities and are therefore unable to graduate from the role of subcontractor to the role of product or brand developer.
- Interviews with apparel manufacturers in Vietnam suggest that, because the manufacturers generally only assemble garments, buyers tend to switch among manufacturers on the basis of costs.

While medium and large firms dominate the sector in China (86 percent), more than 81 percent of firms in the sector in Vietnam are small and medium enterprises (SMEs).[2] The majority of the sectoral workforce in China and Vietnam are women (80 percent); this has important development implications (see chapter 2). The sector generates millions of jobs in China (more than 4.5 million) and in Vietnam (nearly 1.2 million).

The average cost of producing an export-quality polo shirt is about $4.07 in China. Any relevant comparison between China and Vietnam should allow for the cost of raw materials because, in Vietnam, the majority of polo shirt and garment production is assembly only (the CMT method), which does not include raw materials (see above). The cost of raw materials (fabric, collars, thread, and so on) generally constitutes the largest portion of polo shirt production in most countries. China is no exception: raw materials make up 84 percent of the manufacturing costs of polo shirts there. Excluding the raw materials, the production costs in Vietnam compare favorably with those in China (table 4.1). The average cost per polo shirt in Vietnam, excluding raw materials, is $0.48.[3] (The detailed production costs at each stage of the value chain in both countries are shown in figure 4.3 below.)

Table 4.1 Comparative Production Cost of a Polo Shirt, CMT Method, China and Vietnam, 2010

U.S. dollars

China	Vietnam
0.33–0.71	0.39–0.55

Source: GDS 2011.
Note: CMT = cut, make, and trim.

In Vietnam, the availability of good-quality, competitively priced fabric and other raw materials is limited, particularly because the CMT market for imported raw materials developed quickly and without any parallel growth in the local textile industry. With few exceptions, domestic textile producers in Vietnam are unable to satisfy the standards of international buyers in quantity, quality, and timely delivery. However, low (albeit rising) wages and fairly well-developed, business-friendly infrastructure have made Vietnam a prime location for many firms in the Republic of Korea; Taiwan, China; and other places that source garments produced using the CMT method and imported raw materials.

The few Vietnamese manufacturers that export polo shirts tend to be large direct exporters (either foreign-owned firms or state-owned enterprises [SOEs]) that focus mostly on assembly using raw materials supplied from abroad. In China, by contrast, a typical garment manufacturer can choose from thousands of local fabric suppliers, many of them nearby. Once garment designs and order specifications are determined with buyers (foreign or domestic), simple garment orders—those containing one or a few items in small quantities—are delivered to the nearest port in 25–30 days. In Vietnam, deliveries take 45–60 days.

The governments of China and Vietnam provide input and output subsidies to encourage industrial production and exports (table 4.2). Until recently, electricity prices, for example, were controlled and generally subsidized in Vietnam. Industry could obtain electricity at a low price and at rates on a par with those of household consumers without paying premiums for load factors. In China, apparel exporters receive a 16 percent rebate on the exported price of apparel; in other words, all apparel manufacturing value added receives a 16 percent rebate. This more than covers the value added tax manufacturers

Table 4.2 The Apparel Policy and Regulatory Environment, China and Vietnam, 2010

Indicator	China		Vietnam	
	Item	%	Item	% or amount
Tariff	Cotton (preferential)	1–4	Thread (preferential)	5%
	Cotton (regular)	125	Thread (CEPT)	5%
	Fabric (regular)	80–90	Fabric (preferential)	12%
	Fabric (preferential)	10–14	Fabric (CEPT)	5%
	Clothes (regular)	90–130	Clothes (preferential)	20%
	Clothes (preferential)	14.0–17.5	Clothes (CEPT)	5%
Taxes and levies	Value added tax	3 or 17	Value added tax (cotton; other)	5%–10%
	Income tax	25	Income tax	25%
	Other tax	7	Business tax	$55–$155
			Registration fee (land; vehicle)	1%–2%
Subsidies	Export rebate	16	Electricity prices	
			Normal time	$0.047 per kilowatt hour
			Peak time	$0.092 per kilowatt hour
			Off-peak time	$0.025 per kilowatt hour
			Water	$0.351 per cubic meter

Source: GDS 2011.
Note: CEPT = common effective preferential tariff.

pay on inputs and allows Chinese exporters plenty of room for price discounts in their negotiations with foreign buyers.[4]

The Potential

Vietnam is one of the world's largest apparel exporting countries, producing high-quality, low-cost products for the European Union and the United States, for instance. A detailed comparative value chain analysis shows that, if Vietnam can take advantage of various trade arrangements, it has the potential to become more globally competitive in apparel thanks to the following:

- A large, low-wage workforce that is keen to learn. Skilled labor costs in Vietnam are about 57 percent of those in China; unskilled labor costs in Vietnam are 38 percent of the corresponding costs in China.
- Status as a low-cost, high-volume apparel supplier that is internationally price competitive.
- Well-organized enterprises that can produce sophisticated, high-quality items.
- World Trade Organization membership, which facilitates access to new markets and foreign investment.
- A large domestic market of more than 85 million people.
- Relatively cheap utility supply. The prices per unit of electricity, water, and fuel are one-half, one-half to two-thirds, and one-third the respective prices in China, respectively.

Meanwhile, most Chinese apparel factories are located in special economic zones along the coast, in Guangdong, Jiangsu, and Zhejiang provinces. They are predominantly private entities owned by foreign investors.

The most critical challenge facing the apparel industry in China is the increasing difficulty of achieving competitive prices in light of the evolving labor environment. Even with the introduction of social compliance measures, working conditions in China's apparel industry are generally unfavorable.[5] With practically no freedom of association allowed in the country, garment workers, most of whom are migrants from rural areas, move between industries to improve their wages and working conditions. For garment firms, this labor mobility often means high labor turnover rates (up to 85 percent in some parts of Guangdong Province) and mounting labor costs (monthly wages of $200–$300 for unskilled labor in 2010, up 10–20 percent from 2009), resulting in a growing incidence of the inability to accept large orders.

The Main Constraints on Competitiveness

Our value chain analysis has identified key factors affecting the competitiveness of the apparel sector and, in particular, polo shirts in Vietnam.[6] We base the results of our analysis of the sector on 16 firms in China and 8 firms in Vietnam. The most binding constraint is worker skills (figure 4.2). This constraint, along with

Figure 4.2 The Cost to Produce a Polo Shirt in Vietnam Compared with the Cost in China, 2010

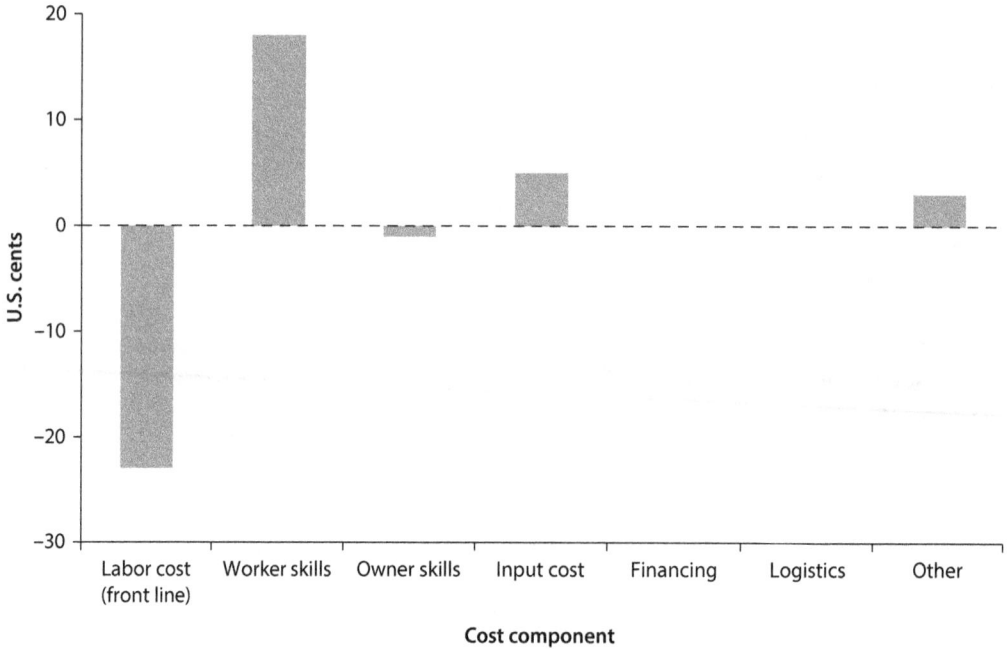

Source: GDS 2011.
Note: Worker skills cover labor efficiency.

higher input prices, wipes out Vietnam's labor cost advantage. Poor labor efficiency accounts for a $0.10–$0.20 cost disadvantage per shirt in Vietnam relative to China. Additionally, while producers in Vietnam manufacture an average of 12 polo shirts per worker per day, garment manufacturers in China's Guangzhou Province produce an average of 25 shirts per worker per day. This outcome may be attributable to the shortage of skilled and semiskilled labor in Vietnam, where there is a perception that jobs in the apparel industry equate with hard work and low compensation. While updated technology may help increase productivity in Vietnam, China's higher productivity is not derived solely from differences in technology; it is also associated with higher skills and greater motivation. For example, in terms of motivation, Chinese workers can save most of their wages because they are provided with inexpensive or free food and housing near the workplace. Even if firms in Vietnam had offered salaries starting at D 2.0 million–D 3.5 million ($104–$181) a month in 2010, they would have had difficulty hiring workers, particularly in the urban and periurban areas where the factories are located. The government is encouraging factories to relocate to rural areas by developing specialized processing zones, but, according to Vinatex, the labor shortage likely exceeded 10 percent in 2010. Despite the country's growing population, labor supply still poses a challenge for apparel enterprises.

The second most binding constraint is input costs. The lack of an integrated value chain means that there is substantial dependence on imported inputs (such as fabrics and accessories), forcing firms to import inputs at high cost, which depresses the amounts firms net on each sale. An estimated 80–90 percent of apparel production in Vietnam relies on imported raw materials (primarily from China; Korea; and Taiwan, China). Most domestic textile producers are incapable of meeting the demand of the apparel sector. Given current production techniques (a significant dependence on rain) and the constantly growing demand for the product (at a rate of 10–15 percent), cotton production in Vietnam has little chance of keeping up with the vibrant textile industry.

Although the soil and weather conditions in Vietnam are good for cotton cultivation, domestic production provides less than 2 percent of the needs of the country's textile and garment industries. It is estimated that Vietnam requires about 400,000 tons of cotton a year to serve these industries, but the country's 12,000 hectares of cotton farmland produce only 5,000 tons. The farmland is limited, and, while there is potential for improvements in yields, the textile and garment industries will still have to rely on cotton imports to remain on a growth path. Because of this constraint, these industries are vulnerable to global price fluctuations—such as in 2010, when global cotton prices more than doubled—and to downward pressures on profits. Thus, if input costs were to surge, the competitive edge associated with Vietnam's low-cost labor advantage would begin to disappear. Our value chain analysis shows that, while the production costs of export-quality polo shirts are lower in Vietnam than in China, Vietnamese producers are unable to capture a higher FOB price relative to their Chinese competitors. This reflects differences in quality; volume; and timely, consistent delivery. Moreover, if Chinese producers are under pressure to sell, they can comfortably reduce their prices in proportion to the export rebate subsidy they obtain from the government (roughly $0.75 per piece at the August 2010 rebate rates). Table 4.3 summarizes the results discussed above in terms of

Table 4.3 Production Cost Breakdown, Polo Shirts, China and Vietnam, 2010
U.S. dollars

Cost component	China	Vietnam
Labor cost, front-line workers	0.40	0.17
Labor efficiency	0	0.18
Capital cost	0.02	0.02
Capital efficiency	0	0
Input cost	3.30	3.35
Input efficiency	0	0
Utility cost and usage	0.02	0.02
Financing cost	0.05	0.05
Trade logistics cost, European Union/United States	0.15	0.15
Overhead and regulatory cost	0.13	0.16
Total cost of production	4.07	4.09
FOB price: quality, delivery, and reputation	5.50	—(CMT)
Net margin	1.43	—

Source: GDS 2011.
Note: — = not applicable; CMT = cut, make, and trim; FOB = free on board.

Table 4.4 Benchmarking Key Production Cost Variables, Polo Shirts, China and Vietnam, 2010

Indicator		China	Vietnam
1.0	*Average spoilage and rejection rate: list different types*		
1.1	In-factory product rejection, %	2–3	1–3
1.2	Product rejection by client, %	0	0–1
2.0	*Average waste and losses: list different types, % of total*		
2.1	Production waste: scrap, fabric-to-polo, weight	5–10	1–7
2.2	Losses, theft	—	0
3.0	*Electricity*		
3.1	On grid, $ per kilowatt hour	0.13	0.07
3.2	Off grid, $ per kilowatt hour, self–generated	—	0.10
3.3	Time off grid per month, %	0–10	7–10
4.0	*Water, $ per cubic meter*	0.59–0.61	0.31–0.45
5.0	*Fuel and oil, $ per liter*	0.87–0.96	0.36–0.87
6.0	*Productivity and efficiency*		
6.1	Range, labor productivity, pieces per employee per day	18–35	8–14
6.2	Average labor productivity, pieces per employee per day	25	12
6.3	Electricity usage, on grid, kilowatt hours per 1,000 pieces	49–196	132–344
6.4	Electricity usage, $ per 1,000 pieces	6–24	8–25
6.5	Water usage, cubic meters per 1,000 pieces	3–14	3–15
6.6	Water usage, $ per 1,000 pieces	2–8	1–7
6.7	Fuel and oil usage, liters per 1,000 pieces	0.5–5.0	1–13
6.8	Fuel and oil usage, $ per 1,000 pieces	1–5	1–13
6.9	Transport, $ per kilometer-tons	0.27–0.30	0.12–0.25

Source: GDS 2011.
Note: Cost in the table reflects assembly only. — = not available.

the advantages and disadvantages of Vietnam and China expressed in U.S. dollars per polo shirt. The average FOB price in China is $5.50, while the average input cost is $3.30. For illustration, Vietnam is assumed to import fabric from Guangdong Province in China.

Table 4.4 provides a detailed benchmarking of key cost components in polo shirt production.[7] Lower labor productivity and the total cost (despite a lower per unit cost) of electricity, fuel, and oil account for most of the disadvantage of Vietnamese production.

While CMT production served Vietnam well during the initial period of industrialization, the slow transformation to original design manufacturing or original brand manufacturing represents a major challenge. CMT is the main attraction for foreign investment, but it also limits the growth of real wages. Any major increase in real wages will cause factories to move abroad without leaving any forward or backward links to the domestic economy. Our survey has found that Vietnamese manufacturers are engaged mainly in the assembly-only production of polo shirts, while relying on imports for the raw materials, a large share of which is provided by the foreign producers placing the orders. This focus on CMT means that Vietnam cannot boost its competitiveness through the production process. If, for example, apparel producers were to establish Vietnamese brands, they could charge more. This margin is currently being forfeited. To realize a fully integrated value chain, from the production of cotton to finished fabric, producers need vast amounts of new investment, technical expertise, and technology. Vinatex recently invested D 15.3 trillion ($800 million) in the production of fiber, cotton, and dye. Nonetheless, achieving growth in the sector requires much more than the level of the investments made by SOEs and private enterprises along the value chain. Whether producers can take the step from the CMT model to original design manufacturing or original brand manufacturing depends on a reorganization of the supply chain (see annex 4A). Channels must be established so that small local producers are able to access inputs and markets abroad either by forming trading companies according to the East Asian model (chapter 3) or by subcontracting with multinational companies.

Because Vietnamese producers rely mainly on the CMT method, a strict comparison of the production cost breakdowns in China and Vietnam is not possible. For this analysis, we therefore simulate the production cost of a polo shirt in Vietnam using imported fabric and assume three markup rates: 10, 20, and 30 percent. Even if we assume a 30 percent markup, producers in Vietnam are still able to achieve a sales price of more than $1 below the price of a polo shirt made in China (figure 4.3). At a 10 percent markup, producers in Vietnam can sell polo shirts for about $1.65 less relative to producers in China.

Other, less important constraints in Vietnam include the following:

- *The excessive use of electricity, water, and fuel.* The significant electricity, water, and fuel usage among producers in Vietnam arises partly—but not entirely—because of the lower utility prices. Thus, although the unit price of utility services in Vietnam is only one-third or one-half the corresponding price in China, Vietnamese firms use more than two or three times the amount of electricity, water, and fuel to produce the same quantity of output, and, for the same output, Vietnamese firms often therefore also pay more for utilities than Chinese firms. One of the main factors behind the excessive use of power may be the older equipment. For example, the equipment used in polo shirt production is generally 4.0–13.0 years old in Vietnam, while it is only 1.1–2.5 years old in China. Furthermore, relatively cheap utilities may not be an advantage for Vietnamese producers much longer. Vietnam is facing more electricity shortages, and investments to raise capacity require higher tariffs to make them financially viable. The government is already planning to introduce market prices for electricity.

- *The difficulties small firms face in gaining access to industrial land and finance.* Despite the Vietnamese government's efforts to support industrial growth, there is no uniform land policy with respect to SMEs. Larger exporters enjoy preferential access to land and financing. The private companies responsible for managing the country's industrial zones favor large manufacturing firms,

Figure 4.3 Cost of Key Production and Margin Items, Polo Shirts, China and Vietnam, 2010

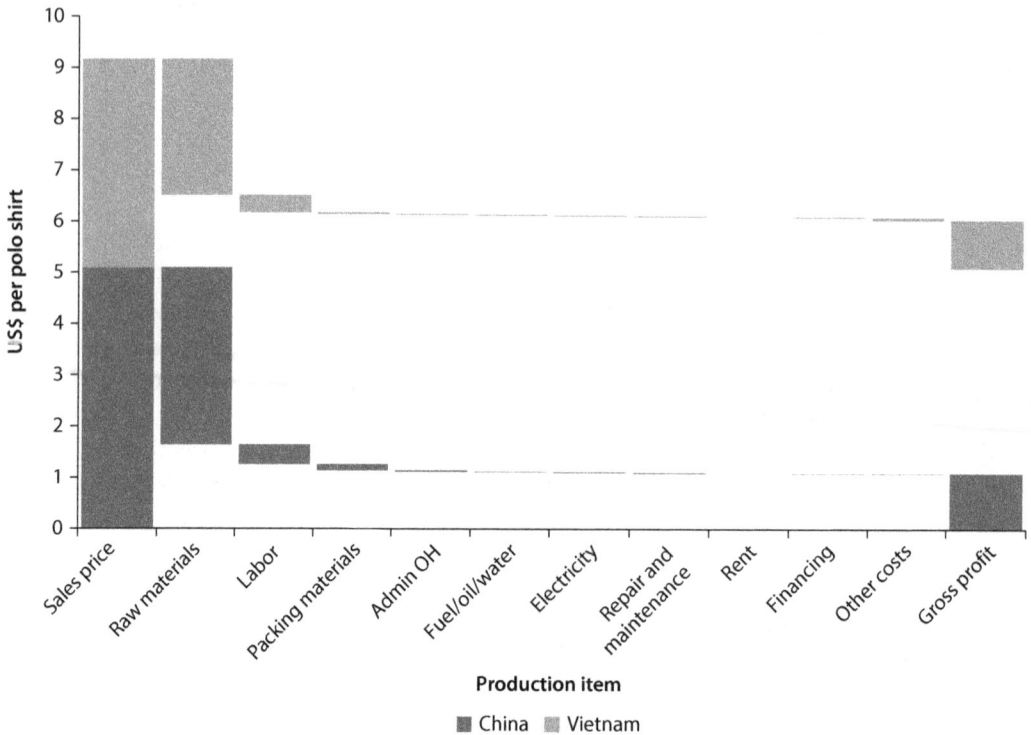

Legend: ■ China ■ Vietnam

Production item

Source: GDS 2011.

Note: The figure is based on the assumption that CMT (cut, make, and trim) producers in Vietnam graduate to full-service FOB (free on board) garment manufacturing; that the raw materials are provided from Guangzhou Province, China; and that there is a 30 percent markup. Admin OH = administration/overhead.

which are usually financed by foreign direct investment (FDI). As in China, these large firms can use extensive facilities in well-designed industrial parks (chapter 3). By contrast, the more restrictive land policies applied to SMEs limit the scope of these enterprises to expand.

Policy Recommendations

Most exporters in Vietnam are limited to low-value CMT activities for which the buyers supply the inputs. Meanwhile, most small domestic firms are trapped in low-productivity, low-value production that caters only to local markets. Our value chain analysis suggests that the costs associated with the CMT production of polo shirts in Vietnam are competitive with the corresponding costs in China. However, without the establishment of a strong, efficient domestic textiles and accessories supply chain in Vietnam, the expansion of export production will not necessarily result in increased domestic content ratios or in value addition. This is why Vietnam continues to have a trade deficit despite robust export growth, and it is why structural and sectoral reforms are so essential for Vietnam's economic development.

The apparel sector urgently requires investments in upstream and down-stream activities. The former—such as fabric and cotton ginning—require skilled labor and, because they are capital intensive, FDI.[8] The latter—especially design and marketing—require technical assistance. Producers must be linked more closely with buyers and suppliers so that they can adapt production designs to meet quality standards and shorten lead times. Because buyers or consolidators currently provide the product and engineering specifications, as well as the production equipment, apparel manufacturers in Vietnam have not developed in-house design and engineering capabilities to allow them to graduate from subcontracting to the development of their own products and brands. There is thus a need for long-term investment strategies in design, marketing, and the creation of new styles. The absence of such strategies is the main reason there are so few well-known Vietnamese fashion brands, even though the country is one of the world's top 10 garment and textile exporters.

Improving worker skills in this sector should be a priority. Experience in other countries shows that labor efficiency and labor quality can be improved through technical assistance programs in well-managed firms. In this case, the efficiency gap would be expected to narrow because of the influx of good-practice companies and good-practice management, regular exposure to global markets, greater capacity utilization, and deeper integration of SMEs with larger firms (chapter 3).

Success also hinges on the ability to create domestic links among enterprises and international links between producers and foreign markets. Measures to create such links include the establishment of trading companies, the fostering of clusters, encouragement for subcontracting, and an increase in social networking through the diaspora community (chapter 3).

To deal with other, less-binding constraints, Vietnam might facilitate access to inputs (besides improving trade logistics) through three sets of measures:

- *Eliminate all import tariffs on apparel inputs.* Duty-free access to inputs is now limited to exporters, and duties are levied on any final goods not exported. Eliminating these duties would enable exporters to resell their material waste (reducing production costs by 1 percent) and facilitate links between large exporters and small domestic producers. The latter would lead to a boost in productivity and in output growth among small players, and it would afford exporters greater flexibility in meeting large orders. See also the discussion on direct and indirect exporters in chapter 3.

- *Reduce the gap in the value chain.* Vietnam could develop a competitive textile industry by taking advantage of its favorable climate and soil conditions for cotton production. This would require encouraging investment in spinning and weaving to reduce import dependence. These industries are intensive in capital, technology, and skills. Therefore, attracting FDI, preferably in partnership with local capital, and strengthening skill training are essential in making these segments of the value chain competitive.

- *Develop plug-and-play industrial parks in areas with input potential.* China has shown that plug-and-play industrial parks can overcome several constraints simultaneously by providing firms with affordable access to industrial land, standardized factory shell buildings, and worker housing, as well as training facilities and one-stop shops for submitting applications, obtaining permits, and meeting other administrative requirements. The parks considerably reduce the financing costs and the risks for efficient smaller firms—which may otherwise be insufficiently large or financially secure to obtain bank loans—so that they are more easily able to grow into medium enterprises. This is how China has avoided the problem of the missing middle. Vietnam does not have a shortage of industrial parks. Indeed, it has too many, and only a few work properly. The key seems to lie in the selection of clusters that would foster forward and backward links among firms, in the encouragement of small firms to move into industrial parks, and in the establishment of an explicit policy to recognize the importance of large private sector manufacturing firms.

Vietnam can seek to develop competitive clusters wherein large firms can connect with small firms. The CMT method has provided Vietnamese garment producers with opportunities to strengthen operational and management capacity without committing scarce resources or taking risks, but these producers are now in a position to make investments to reach the next level of competitiveness. The cluster links among firms would be beneficial for large exporters and would help them succeed.

Annex 4A: Shifting from CMT to FOB Manufacturing in Polo Shirts

Table 4A.1 illustrates a scenario in which Vietnam garment assembly firms operate under the most basic FOB arrangement. In this scenario, buyers designate the raw material supplier or suppliers, and the Vietnamese firms then source fabric and other raw materials on their own.[9] Under such terms and if we assume that the current market price for transportation from Guangzhou Province, China, to Hanoi is $650 per 20-foot-equivalent unit, including all handling and overland transport charges in Vietnam, a typical Vietnamese firm could potentially source fabric at $1.82 per polo shirt and other raw materials at $0.57 per polo shirt. If material, transportation, estimated overhead, and other manufacturing costs (including labor) are added, Vietnamese firms could potentially produce export-quality polo shirts that are similar to those highlighted in the value chain analysis at a cost of $3.13 per piece.

At a production cost of $3.13 per polo shirt, Vietnamese firms would be able to compete internationally in price.[10] This, however, does not necessarily mean that Vietnamese firms should immediately abandon the CMT production method and initiate the shift toward an FOB method, especially the more complex FOB arrangements (types II and III). The complex FOB arrangements— whereby buyers send samples and the Vietnamese firms find their own suppliers or whereby Vietnamese firms initiate garment production based on their own

Table 4A.1 FOB Production Cost of a Polo Shirt in Vietnam with Fabric Imported from China
U.S. dollars

Cost component	Estimate per shirt
Fabric, FOB Guangzhou, China[a]	1.82
Other material, FOB Guangzhou, China[a]	0.57
Sea freight, customs clearance, and related charges, Guangzhou–Hanoi[b]	0.03
Overhead: supply chain management, financing, and related costs, 10% of raw material cost	0.23
Other manufacturing costs, including labor[c]	0.48
Total cost, FOB Hanoi	3.13

Source: GDS 2011.
Note: FOB = free on board.
a. Based on prices in Guangzhou, less value added tax charts for local sales in China.
b. Includes overland transport and other charges in Vietnam. Assumes no duties in Vietnam.
c. Average among firms at which interviews were conducted in Vietnam.

designs—generally require significant financing to build and organize the relevant supply chain and design capabilities, and they also take time. The CMT strategy, which is built on steady labor costs and productive competitiveness, should be abandoned only after careful measurement of the costs associated with the more complex supply chain management required under FOB types II and III.

Notes

1. CMT refers to a form of garment production whereby the apparel manufacturer is provided with all inputs by the foreign buyer or consolidator and performs only the cutting, assembly, and trim of the garment. In FOB garment production, the apparel manufacturer is responsible for all production activities, including the procurement (sourcing and financing) of the raw materials, piece goods, and trim; the CMT functions; and finishing. FOB, in this context, signifies that the buyers and consolidators do not supply inputs and take delivery of final goods produced by the manufacturer. For a more detailed description of the sector in Vietnam, see Pham and others (2013).

2. For this report, the specifications of firms are based on GDS (2011). The most appropriate comparison for the sectors in this study involves the classification according to the industrial type system in China, where small enterprises have fewer than 300 employees, earn less than Y 30 million, and have less than Y 40 million in assets, and medium enterprises have 300–2,000 employees, Y 30 million–Y 300 million in revenue, and Y 40 million–Y 400 million in assets. In Vietnam, small firms have fewer than 50 employees, and medium firms have 51–200 employees. Within these classifications, there are more detailed categories, such as super small firms (fewer than 10 employees).

3. In the production scheme in Vietnam, local manufacturers are expected to cover all production costs, including equipment maintenance and packaging materials, while buyers provide the raw materials.

4. The rebate rates and the list of items that qualify for export rebates change frequently depending on the assessments by policy makers of various trends, such as the global price outlook and local market developments.

5. For example, the CSC9000t—China Social Compliance 9000 for the Textile and Apparel Industry—code of conduct for the textile and apparel industry was

introduced in 2005 by the China National Textile and Apparel Council. The code is still new, and, proportionally, only a small number of firms are involved. Also, the code is not compulsory, nor is it independently verified.

6. For a note on the methodology behind our value chain analysis, see appendix A.

7. Value chain diagrams in this section reflect data from export-oriented best practice firms.

8. For example, in 2009, it cost about $3 million–$5 million to build a large garment factory, but a weaving mill cost $12 million–$25 million and a spinning mill $50 million–$70 million, a huge amount for any garment factory owner. See Birnbaum (2009).

9. The operations known as FOB by Vietnamese firms and firms in some other countries vary significantly in the contractual relationships with foreign buyers. Such operations may be classified into three main types. In the first type, FOB type I, the Vietnamese firms purchase input materials from suppliers designated by the foreign buyers. In the second type, FOB type II, the Vietnamese firms receive garment samples from the foreign buyers and proceed on their own to establish the necessary input arrangements. In the third type, FOB type III, the Vietnamese firms initiate the production of garments based on their own designs without any prior commitment from foreign buyers. We consider only FOB type I in our example here.

10. This production cost estimate is based on the assumption that the Vietnamese firms are required by their clients to source fabric and other materials from Chinese suppliers similar to those supplying the Chinese firms examined in the value chain analysis. This scenario is hypothetical and should not be used as a basis for investment decisions, especially in regard to the price of fabric. Dedicated suppliers (those qualifying as suppliers of choice among big brand retailers) generally charge a premium for their materials because of the connection with the existing supply chain of big buyers. This issue is not considered in our scenario.

References

Birnbaum, David. 2009. "Analysis: The New Garment Supplier: Where, Who, What (Part II)." just-style.com, May 26. http://www.just-style.com/comment/where-who-what-part-ii_id104250.aspx.

GDS (Global Development Solutions). 2011. *The Value Chain and Feasibility Analysis; Domestic Resource Cost Analysis.* Vol. 2 of *Light Manufacturing in Africa: Targeted Policies to Enhance Private Investment and Create Jobs.* Washington, DC: World Bank. http://go.worldbank.org/6G2A3TFI20.

Pham, Duc Minh, Deepak Mishra, Kee-Cheok Cheong, John Arnold, Anh Minh Trinh, Huyen Thi Ngoc Ngo, and Hien Thi Phuong Nguyen. 2013. *Trade Facilitation, Value Creation, and Competitiveness: Policy Implications for Vietnam's Economic Growth.* Vol. 2. Hanoi: World Bank.

CHAPTER 5

Leather

Vietnam's leather industry is strongly export oriented. However, most of the exporters are foreign-owned companies; domestic companies produce mainly for the local market. Most enterprises perform only final assembly. Foreign buyers supply the inputs and designs. Labor costs are low and highly competitive, but the majority of workers have no professional skills or expertise. Consequently, labor productivity is low, particularly relative to China. Another constraint is the lack of input industries. Inputs must be imported. Electricity and water costs are high mainly because of waste, inefficiency, and, thus, poor management. The skilled labor shortage could be addressed through training and by facilitating rural-urban migration. The use of new sources of imported leather, such as Ethiopian leather, would help cut input costs. Local design and the technical capabilities necessary to develop local product lines should be fostered. Foreign direct investment (FDI) should be encouraged to focus on the early stages of production, such as tanning. Import tariffs on leather inputs should be reduced and then removed.

Description of the Sector

Leather footwear and leather products account for approximately 40 percent of the value of industrial production in Vietnam and nearly 10 percent of the country's export turnover. On an annual basis, Vietnam produces more than 800 million pairs of leather shoes, 120 million leather bags, and 150 million square feet of tanned leather products, of which more than 90 percent are exported. The country is one of the world's largest leather footwear producers and exporters. The global industry in footwear with leather uppers had a record export value of $47.9 billion in 2008. In 2009, more than $40 billion in leather products were traded. China, the largest exporter ($8.3 billion), accounted for 19.8 percent of the global market, followed by Italy ($6.8 billion, or 16.1 percent), and Vietnam ($2.3 billion, or 7.9 percent) (figure 5.1).

According to the Vietnam Leather and Footwear Association, the country's leather sector employed approximately 632,000 workers in 2009. Because much

Figure 5.1 Leading Exporters of Footwear with Leather Uppers, Worldwide, 2009

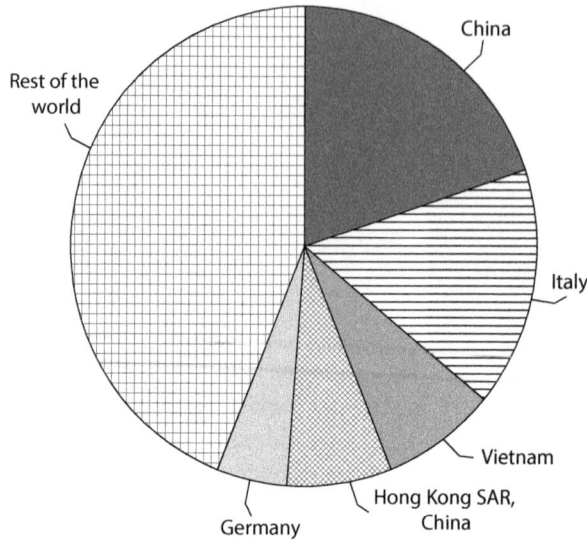

Source: GDS 2011.

of the leather shoe production is carried out through subcontracts, the sector is represented fairly evenly by small, medium, and large enterprises. Small firms account for 51 percent of the leather products in Vietnam, compared with 40 percent in China. The composition of the workforce directly employed in the production of leather products differs between the two countries: 55 percent of the workers in China are men, while, in Vietnam, the industry is dominated by women (82 percent).

As a reference point in our analysis, we use men's leather loafers and the performance of a representative sample of 14 firms in China and 12 firms in Vietnam. Like the apparel industry, leather is strongly export oriented. Although the largest share of companies in the industry in Vietnam are small, most of the exporters are large and either foreign-owned or state-owned enterprises (SOEs). Half of Vietnam's shoe exports are generated by one foreign-owned producer, while most domestic companies produce shoes only for the domestic market.[1] Also similar to the apparel sector, most leather and footwear enterprises in Vietnam operate under contracts as product processors. Foreign buyers (the contractors) provide the inputs and designs, and Vietnamese firms provide the cheap labor and are responsible for processing. Foreign partners are also responsible for marketing the finished product and the high–value added stages of the supply chain.

Of the 819 officially registered enterprises in the production of leather shoes in 2010, 235 (28.7 percent) were partially or wholly foreign owned,

77 (9.4 percent) were private domestic enterprises, and 507 (61.9 percent) were SOEs. Almost all the large enterprises are partially or wholly foreign owned.

The cost of producing export-quality men's sheepskin loafers in China is about $16.17 per pair ($9.39 per pair for the local market).[2] In Vietnam, as in the apparel sector, a large majority of shoe production involves only final assembly ($1.75 a pair), and the input materials (usually with the exception of packaging materials and the process of packing) are provided by the buyers. This masks the cost of the raw material (the sheepskin), which generally constitutes the largest portion of the cost of such shoe production. In China, the average cost associated with all raw materials required for the production of export-quality loafers accounts for about 36 percent of the total value. A production cost comparison with Vietnam is therefore not straightforward because of Vietnam's cut, make, and trim (CMT) mode of production.

Our value chain and supply chain analyses reveal that Vietnamese producers in the leather shoe industry are highly competitive, thanks mainly to low labor costs (table 5.1).

Vietnam's success thus far has hinged on its ability to take advantage of cheap labor. Compared with China, this advantage is considerable and appears to outweigh disadvantages in the other costs associated with leather shoe production (figure 5.2). Additionally, there is potential to improve productivity in Vietnam.

Why has Vietnam not yet expanded its global share in this market segment? And why has there not been a greater flow of investment into the sector? The answers revolve around low productivity as a result of poor labor skills and poor production line management. These issues can be addressed through training and capacity building.

However, input industries must be established, and this takes time. One lesson of production in China is that large-volume production does not necessarily require large-scale production facilities. It can be achieved while remaining fairly small by limiting overhead costs and improving equipment and labor use rates.

Meanwhile, low transport costs and low utility prices contribute significantly to the low unit production cost of loafer shoes in Vietnam. The per-unit price of water is about one-half to two-thirds relative to China, and the per-unit price of fuel is around one-third relative to China. Despite the cheaper unit price, the electricity bills of Vietnamese firms are two or three times higher than those of

Table 5.1 CMT Production Costs, Sheepskin Loafers, China and Vietnam, 2010
U.S. dollars

China	Vietnam
1.73–6.81	1.30–2.96

Source: GDS 2011.

Figure 5.2 The Cost to Produce a Pair of Leather Shoes in Vietnam Compared with the Cost in China, 2010

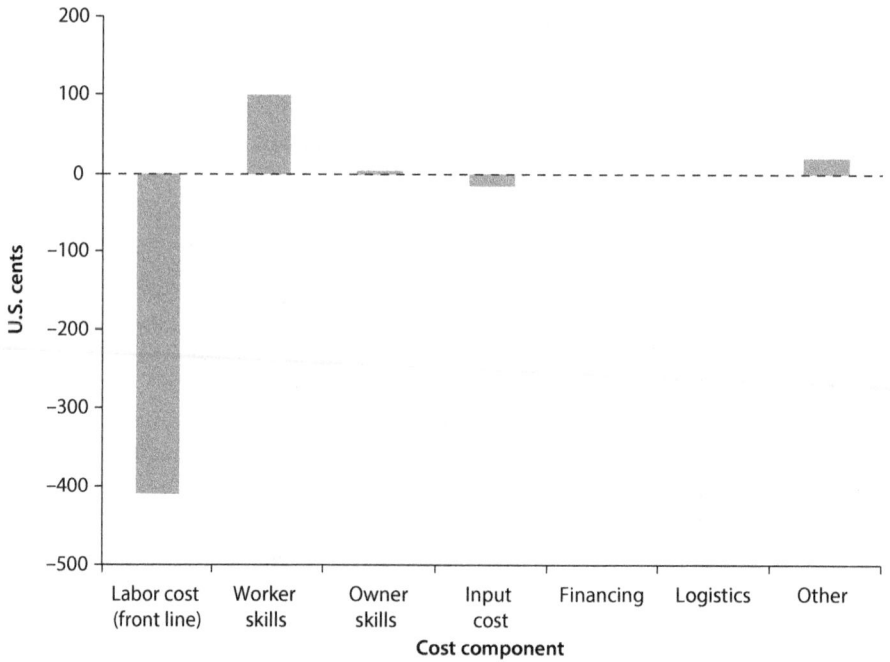

Source: GDS 2011.
Note: Worker skills cover labor efficiency.

Chinese firms. Firms in Vietnam use five times the electricity of their counterparts in China. A similar situation prevails in the use of water. Total electricity and water costs are higher mainly because of waste, inefficiency, and poor management. Equipment is also much older and more outdated in Vietnam relative to China (table 5.2).[3]

While Vietnamese producers are competitive because of lower wages, the leather sector relies heavily on imported raw materials and lags behind China in market position in major European Union and U.S. markets. A more in-depth assessment of best practice firms in China and Vietnam provides insight into the challenges facing Vietnamese firms. Similar to polo shirt producers, exporters of leather shoes in Vietnam tend to be large and are either foreign owned or SOEs. Private sector producers work mainly as subcontractors of large companies. In this sense, they are more well integrated than similar producers in the apparel sector. Nonetheless, all foreign-owned, state-owned, and domestic producers rely on imported raw materials because of the lack of support industries. This weakens the leather shoe industry's supply chain in many ways, including timely deliveries, and therefore reduces profitability.

Table 5.2 Benchmarking Key Variables in Leather Loafer Production, China and Vietnam

Indicator	China	Vietnam
Factory		
Capacity utilization, %	90	60–98
Installed capacity, pieces per day	350–650	5,000–20,000
Labor absenteeism rate, %	1	2
Average monthly salary or wage, $		
Skilled	296–562	119–140
Unskilled	237–488	78–93
Days of operation per month	26–28	25–29
Average age of major equipment, years	3.0–5.3	4.7–10.0
Exported output, finished primary product		
Direct export without consolidator or broker, %	0	100
Indirect export through local consolidator, %	0–100	0
Indirect export through overseas consolidator, %	0	0
Domestically sold output, finished primary product		
Direct sales to wholesalers and retailers without consolidators, %	0–100	0
Direct sales through own outlets, shops, or showrooms, %	0	0
Indirect sales through local consolidator or trader, %	0	0
Unit production cost, per piece	$9.39–$16.17	$1.30–$3.04[a]
Average selling price, $		
Factory gate	11.54–19.82	—
Wholesale	12.03–20.86	—
Free on board	4.05–21.75	3.63–4.92

Source: GDS 2011.
Note: — = not applicable.
a. The data for Vietnam reflect assembly costs only.

The Potential

Vietnam's performance is as promising in leather products as it is in apparel. Its potential in the leather product industry stems from a number of factors:

- Vietnamese workers cost less to employ. Relative to China, skilled labor costs less than half ($119–$140 a month), and unskilled labor costs less than a third ($78–$93 a month).
- Vietnam has a 25 percent production cost advantage over China because of its lower-cost labor and because the leather sector is even more labor intensive than the apparel sector. In China, labor accounts for 40 percent of the total production cost in the leather product industry, compared with only 10 percent in apparel.
- Vietnam's increasing integration in world trade, including through the Association of Southeast Asian Nations, the World Trade Organization, and the negotiations for the Trans-Pacific Partnership (TPP), represents a significant

opportunity for the leather industry to access new and advanced technologies, as well as larger markets.[4] While the industry must follow certain binding rules imposed by these organizations, it also enjoys enhanced economic cooperation and fair treatment through membership. The sector now faces fierce competition from leather and footwear producers in the region and elsewhere.
- As in the apparel sector, the domestic market for leather products in Vietnam is large and growing. Nonetheless, on the demand side, of the 130 million pairs of shoes absorbed by the domestic market, more than 70 percent are accounted for by shoe imports rather than by local manufacturers.

The Main Constraints on Competitiveness

Leather and footwear are a major contributor to the Vietnamese economy, but leather and footwear enterprises face a number of challenges in the country, many of which are similar to those faced by enterprises in the apparel sector. To maintain its competitive price advantage over rivals in China, India, and Thailand, the industry in Vietnam must address the following challenges:

- The lower relative productivity arising because of the shortage of low-cost, semiskilled labor
- The fact that more than 70 percent of raw materials and other inputs are imported
- The lack of local design and technical capability to develop independent brands and product lines; most of the technology and methods used in shoe production in Vietnam are being implemented by foreign-owned original equipment manufacturers
- The rising local labor costs

The most binding constraint in the industry is the lack of professional skills and expertise in leather goods production among the majority of the workers in the sector. Consequently, labor productivity is lower in Vietnam than in other countries in the region, particularly China. In Vietnam, a worker typically makes 1.3–5.8 pairs of shoes a day, while a Chinese worker produces 3.0–7.2 pairs of shoes a day. Poor labor productivity is clearly the main obstacle in the production process. The wage differential between skilled and unskilled workers is only 14 percent in China, but, in Vietnam, the difference is 34 percent. While there may be a shortage of unskilled workers in China, the marginal difference in wage rates suggests that even unskilled workers in China require less supervision than their counterparts in Vietnam.

The leather sector in Vietnam is also limited by the fact that, similar to the apparel sector, such a large share of the input needs must be filled by imports. This means that the industry is vulnerable to market fluctuations in price and availability that can cut into profits. The industry must address this issue in the short to medium term. The domestic cattle industry, which could be an ideal source of hides, is busy meeting the significant demand among footwear enterprises. The country lacks large-scale cattle farms; most domestic raw leather is purchased from slaughterhouses and rural households. Despite the high demand for leather, the local tanning industry is hindered by outdated equipment and a shortage of investment capital. Domestic tanneries are unable to provide leather in any quantity approaching the requirements even of shoe manufacturers alone. As a result, quality leather will have to be imported in the foreseeable future.

Box 5.1 demonstrates that the use of Ethiopian leather as an input could help the industry in Vietnam reduce input costs and become more globally competitive.

Low local content rates and limited local branding and product development represent additional constraints on the leather sector. Similar to the apparel industry, the leather industry is forgoing a great deal of profit that could be obtained with extra effort. Improving productivity and capturing a greater

---

Box 5.1 Can Vietnam Be Competitive in Leather Using Sheepskin Imported from Ethiopia?

If the quality of the sheepskin Ethiopia produces could be improved and the production of finished skins could be expanded to a level approximating the country's supply of animals, could it become a major exporter of sheepskin, and could countries such as Vietnam take advantage of such high-quality, low-cost skins?

A simulated cost estimate for the production of sheepskin loafers using input material only from China or using sheepskin from Ethiopia, combined with other input material from China, suggests that Vietnam could become a competitive producer of sheepskin loafers using sheepskin from Ethiopia (table B5.1.1).

Table B5.1.1 Two Production Cost Estimates Using Imported Inputs, Sheepskin Loafers, Vietnam

U.S. dollars

Inputs imported exclusively from China			Inputs imported from Ethiopia and China
Freight: Guangzhou, China, to Hanoi via Hai Phong port (estimate)	650	2,944	Freight: Addis Ababa to Hanoi via Djibouti and Hai Phong port (estimate)
Transport cost, pair (estimate)	0.09	0.39	Transport cost, pair (estimate)
Sheepskin, $ per pair	5.85	3.72	Sheepskin from Ethiopia, $ per pair
Other inputs, with transport, $ per pair	3.36	3.45	Other inputs from China, with transport, $ per pair
Input cost, with transport, pair (estimate)	9.30	7.55	Input cost, with transport, pair (estimate)
Assembly cost in best practice factory in Vietnam	1.75	1.75	Assembly cost in best practice factory in Vietnam
Cost, pair (estimate)	11.05	9.30	Cost, pair (estimate)

Source: GDS 2011.

share of sales will be critical in curbing rising labor prices, which will certainly have a negative effect on the competitiveness of leather and footwear products over time.

Other challenges in the future will likely revolve around environmental protection and worker rights. Large companies such as Nike have recently made commitments in these areas.[5] Demands for the use of energy-saving, environmentally friendly technologies in China have emerged as foreign governments impose increasingly tighter restrictions on the use of certain chemical substances in leather processing. The ability to be flexible and adapt to these pressures will be decisive as production standards evolve.

Policy Recommendations

Vietnam is currently one of the world's most attractive investment destinations mainly because of low labor costs. Rising wages are, of course, a desirable goal of development in any country and should be encouraged, but, unless the issue of the growth and integration of domestic companies is addressed, the country could become locked into a vicious circle: rising real wages could easily lead to job losses if production facilities move abroad. Hence, policy makers must walk a fine line between raising wages and maintaining employment. It is therefore crucial to address the problems of the numerous small household enterprises producing for the domestic market as well as the problems faced by a relatively small number of modern, foreign-invested enterprises producing for export. To become more competitive, especially in the face of the challenges, the leather industry must capture greater profits, increase productivity, and source cheaper inputs. Furthermore, the labor shortage could be addressed through training and by facilitating rural-urban migration by, for example, formally abolishing the *ho khau* system, the household registration system used to verify the legal status of a person within the country, including urban or rural residence. Raising productivity will help shield workers if wages rise too high too quickly.

Shifting away from CMT, as in the apparel sector, is key if the leather industry is to remain competitive. This will require the introduction of local design and initiatives to instill the technical capabilities necessary to develop local brands and product lines. The lack of local design is a weakness that the leather and footwear industry must overcome to achieve sustainable growth.

Perhaps more importantly, the majority of companies—more than 60 percent—are small and medium enterprises (SMEs) producing for the domestic market; they do not compete in the world market. These enterprises are characterized by low production efficiency and huge output fluctuations. Integration with world markets would allow these producers to gain access to a wider range of inputs and markets.

Leather processing requires good-quality raw materials and access to credit, skills, and technology. Facilitating the import of high-quality processed leather in the short term and the development of a competitive leather supply chain in the long term would position Vietnam to become one of the leading global centers in the production of quality leather goods. Policies to enhance the value chain in this area should aim at encouraging FDI—preferably in cooperation with local companies—that is focused on the early stages of production, such as tanning, because these stages tend to be capital intensive and require highly skilled labor that can be developed only over time.

Meanwhile, policies that penalize the import of inputs and the export of final goods should be reevaluated to create greater incentives for producers to source inputs domestically or from countries such as Ethiopia. For some shoe parts, tariffs are now as high as 30 percent in Vietnam (and up to 20 percent in China). Vietnam seems to bear a higher tax burden, particularly because there is no value added tax refund as in China. Import tariffs on leather inputs for both direct and indirect exporters should therefore be reduced and eventually removed. This would help domestic producers expand production.

Other policy recommendations include the following:

- *Promote advocacy and technical assistance.* It is essential that sectoral associations advocate for member interests in dialogue with the government and other stakeholders. These associations can also provide services to members, such as training and information sharing. The institutional capacity and financial resources of these associations are currently limited.
- *Spur the emergence of clusters in the leather industry.* This can be facilitated by developing specific industrial zones for the sector (chapter 3). This should be supplemented by training in entrepreneurship and in management, technical, and design skills.
- *Commercialize the livestock industry.* This would help improve the health of livestock, the quality of hides and skins, and the offtake ratio.[6] Encouraging the establishment of modern abattoirs in appropriate locations would significantly improve the offtake ratio. Such upstream measures would enhance quality at every stage in the value chain.
- *Enhance extension services.* Even if livestock is commercialized, the majority of production units will remain smallholders for the foreseeable future. To assist these smallholders, extension services need to be substantially improved, particularly in crossbreeding, disease control, and training in slaughtering techniques; preservation practices; quality control; and the potential value of hides and skins.

Notes

1. For example, see "Vietnam Top Choice for Nike Footwear," December 24, 2011, Malaysian National News Agency, http://vics.vn/vics-news/economic-investment/1237/vietnam-top-choice-for-nike-footwear.aspx.

2. While the technical specifications of products from China, Ethiopia, and Vietnam are the same, we have noted quality differences, particularly with regard to the

finish and the stitching. Furthermore, the loafer styles also vary greatly across the samples we have examined.

3. A number of large footwear assembly facilities—at more than 100,000 square meters and with more than 14,000 workers—are active in Vietnam.

4. As of December 2013, the Trans-Pacific Partnership countries, either currently negotiating membership or signatories, were Australia, Brunei Darussalam, Canada, Chile, Japan, Malaysia, Mexico, New Zealand, Peru, Singapore, the United States, and Vietnam.

5. "We will be moving away from companies that are not committed to putting workers and sustainability at the heart of their growth agendas," said Hannah Jones, a representative of Nike, in a telephone interview quoted in Townsend (2012). "There are new rules of engagement."

6. The offtake ratio is the ratio of the number of animals slaughtered over a given period (generally a year) to the total size of the herd at a given time (the number of head of livestock).

References

GDS (Global Development Solutions). 2011. *The Value Chain and Feasibility Analysis; Domestic Resource Cost Analysis.* Vol. 2 of *Light Manufacturing in Africa: Targeted Policies to Enhance Private Investment and Create Jobs.* Washington, DC: World Bank. http://go.worldbank.org/6G2A3TFI20.

Townsend, Matt. 2012. "Nike Raises Factory Labor and Sustainability Standards." Bloomberg, May 3. http://www.bloomberg.com/news/2012-05-03/nike-raises-factory -labor-and-sustainability-standards.html.

CHAPTER 6

Wood Products

As in other light manufacturing industries, abundant low-cost labor is a clear strength of the wood processing industry in Vietnam. Other advantages include diverse and expanding markets and better value relative to producers in other countries. The most binding constraint is the low productivity in Vietnam, which is due partly to the limited training and experience of managers and line workers and partly to low capacity use and the excessive consumption of inputs, mainly because of inefficiency, poor management, and old equipment. Similar to the apparel and leather sectors, producers of wood products do not participate much in product development, leading to skill deficiencies in design, branding, marketing, human resource management, and the sourcing of raw materials. Other binding constraints include the rising costs of and significant reliance on imported timber, the lack of access to land suitable for production-related operations, and the expanding regulatory framework governing environmentally friendly methods and the sourcing of wood. Vocational training, Kaizen training, and technical assistance would help address the shortages in skilled labor and management. Plug-and-play industrial parks should also be developed, and new investment and technology upgrades should be encouraged.

Description of the Sector

In 2009, the value of the international trade in wood and wood products totaled $90 billion, down $20 billion from 2008 and down $35 billion from the 2007 peak.[1] The largest exporters of wood and wood products in 2009 were Germany ($8.5 billion) and China ($7.7 billion), while the leading exporters of wood furniture, lighting, prefabricated buildings, and parts were also China and Germany (figure 6.1).

Vietnam has been one of the few countries among the top global exporters of wood products that has increased exports in the face of the downturn in global demand. The country is the second-largest Asian exporter of wood furniture, lighting, and prefabricated buildings. In 2009, the value of its wood product exports was $3.4 billion, ninth highest in the world. At the current rate of export growth, Vietnam is soon likely to move up to sixth place, overtaking

Figure 6.1 Leading Exporters of Wood Furniture, Lighting, Prefabricated Buildings, and Parts, Worldwide, 2009

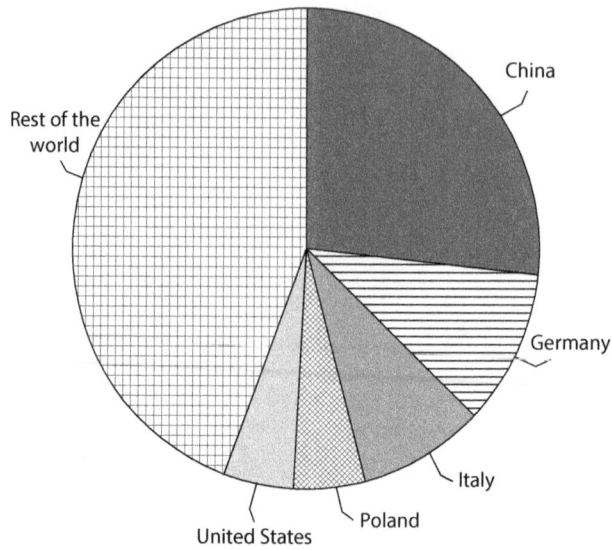

Source: GDS 2011.

Table 6.1 The Wood Processing Industry, China and Vietnam, 2009

Indicator	China	Vietnam
Total imports, value, $	7,533,118,000	569,632,000
Wood and articles of wood	7,255,434,000	545,541,000
Wooden furniture	277,684,000	24,091,000
Total exports, value, $	19,783,674,000	3,336,110,000
Wood and articles of wood	7,713,472,000	625,574,000
Wooden furniture	12,070,202,000	2,710,536,000
Companies, total	10,314	2,389
Small, %	14	32
Medium, %	56	65
Large, %	30	2
Workers, total (estimate)	1,360,248	107,536
Men, %	67	48
Women, %	33	52

Sources: GDS 2011; UN Comtrade (United Nations Commodity Trade Statistics Database), Statistics Division, Department of Economic and Social Affairs, United Nations, New York, http://comtrade.un.org/db/; labor data taken from national statistics.
Note: The data on China includes only firms with annual turnover of more than Y 5 million.

powerhouses Canada and Mexico. Vietnam has much smaller operations: only 1/12 the sectoral employment and barely a quarter the number of firms in China (table 6.1). Nonetheless, it has managed to achieve about a sixth of the value of the exports of China. This is impressive and highlights the growth potential of wood processing in the Vietnamese economy.

We base the results of our analysis of the sector on 16 firms in China and 12 firms in Vietnam. We use wooden chairs as the reference product.

The Potential

The wood sector is one of Vietnam's top 10 export earners and is a significant contributor to gross domestic product (GDP). Vietnam's comparative advantages in the sector include the following:

- A low-cost workforce: The labor force is diligent, hardworking, and keen to learn. Vietnam has one of the world's lowest industrial wage structures.
- Competitive production costs: The wood processing industry is labor intensive; so, production costs are highly competitive.
- Diverse and expanding markets: Vietnam's accession to the World Trade Organization, combined with participation in free trade agreements, has helped grow the country's export markets. Economic growth has also fueled domestic demand.
- Good value: The quality and the competitive prices of Vietnamese products relative to the equivalent products of other Asian countries are attractive.

The Main Constraints on Competitiveness

The impressive growth in Vietnam's processed wood products industry over the past several years has overshadowed the corresponding growth in Indonesia, Malaysia, and Thailand in export markets, but Vietnam faces critical challenges. The most binding constraints are best illustrated by furniture production costs. The average cost to produce a wooden chair is $17.50 in Vietnam, but only $13.53 in China.[2] The price difference is huge if one considers that the inputs are much less expensive in Vietnam, where lumber costs are only about 40 percent of the costs in China. Even if the inputs are imported in Vietnam, they are still about $100 cheaper per cubic meter than corresponding inputs in China (table 6.2). This is surprising given that wood is a low value-to-weight item. However, it highlights Vietnam's input price advantage over China.

Lumber is significantly more expensive in China than in Vietnam; so, the reason for the nearly $4 higher production cost per chair in Vietnam can be narrowed mainly to low labor productivity and the excessive use of other inputs. The average number of chairs produced per worker per day is 4.5 in China, but only 1.9 in Vietnam.[3] The low overall productivity in Vietnam arises because of the limited training and experience of managers and line workers and is associated with low capacity use (60–80 percent in most furniture and seat manufacturing firms). Vietnam spends more on inputs, such as electricity, especially during framing and assembly. Even if we control for the considerably cheaper utility prices, Vietnam spends significantly more than China (table 6.3). One reason is that the production equipment is almost two times older in Vietnam relative to China.

Table 6.2 The Price of a Cubic Meter of Pine Lumber, China, Ethiopia, and Vietnam, 2010

U.S. dollars

Country	Imported	Domestic
China	n.a.	344
Ethiopia	n.a.	667
Vietnam	246	146

Source: GDS 2011.
Note: Domestic denotes the origin of the supplier, but not necessarily the source of the wood.
n.a. = not applicable.

Table 6.3 Benchmarking Key Production Variables, Wooden Chairs, China and Vietnam, 2010

Indicator	China	Vietnam
Average waste and losses		
Lumber-to-chair conversion, % of waste	10	5–35
Electricity		
On grid, $ per kilowatt hour	0.13–0.15	0.08
Off grid, self-generated, $ per kilowatt hour	—	0.13
Time off grid, % per month	0–14	0–4
Water		
$ per square meter	0.44–0.47	0.26
Fuel and oil		
$ per 1,000 pieces	13.39–26.55	13.75–26.22
Productivity and efficiency		
Labor productivity, wooden chairs, pieces per employee per day	3.0–6.0	1.2–2.6
Electricity use, on grid, kilowatt hours per 1,000 pieces	682–1,190	8,800–28,500
Electricity use, on grid, $ per 1,000 pieces	90.57–175.59	468.00–2,220.00
Water use, square meters per 1,000 pieces	58.64–83.33	25.00–67.00
Water use, $ per 1,000 pieces	25.19–39.33	3.40–16.84
Fuel and oil use, liters per 1,000 pieces	14.2–27.5	17.0–52.0
Fuel and oil use, $ per 1,000 pieces	13.39–26.55	13.75–26.22
Transport, $ per kilometer-ton	0.12–0.28	0.10–0.18

Source: GDS 2011.
Note: — = not available.

These inefficiencies are compounded by the excessive use of glue (61 grams per chair in Vietnam, but only 44 grams in China) and varnish, which end up costing 50 percent per chair more in Vietnam than in China (table 6.4). Some of these differences in input use may be explained by consumer preferences in the local Vietnamese markets for, say, heavy oil or varnish finishes. However, the significant use of these consumables also points to poor management and the lack of worker skills in furniture manufacturing and reinforces the findings related to low labor productivity. The relevant expertise must be increased if the international competitiveness of Vietnamese furniture manufacturing is to be strengthened.

Table 6.4 Benchmarking Manufacturing Costs, Wooden Chairs, China and Vietnam, 2010

	China			Vietnam		
Consumables	$/kg	Grams/chair	$/chair	$/kg	Grams/chair	$/chair
Adhesives, glues	2.21	44	0.10	3.24	61	0.20
Varnish, finishing oils	5.10	50	0.25	7.54	112	0.84
Other consumables	—	—	0.16	—	—	0.44
Total	—	—	0.51	—	—	1.48

Source: GDS 2011.
Note: — = not available; kg = kilogram.

Figure 6.2 Cost of Key Production and Margin Items, Wooden Chairs, China and Vietnam, 2010

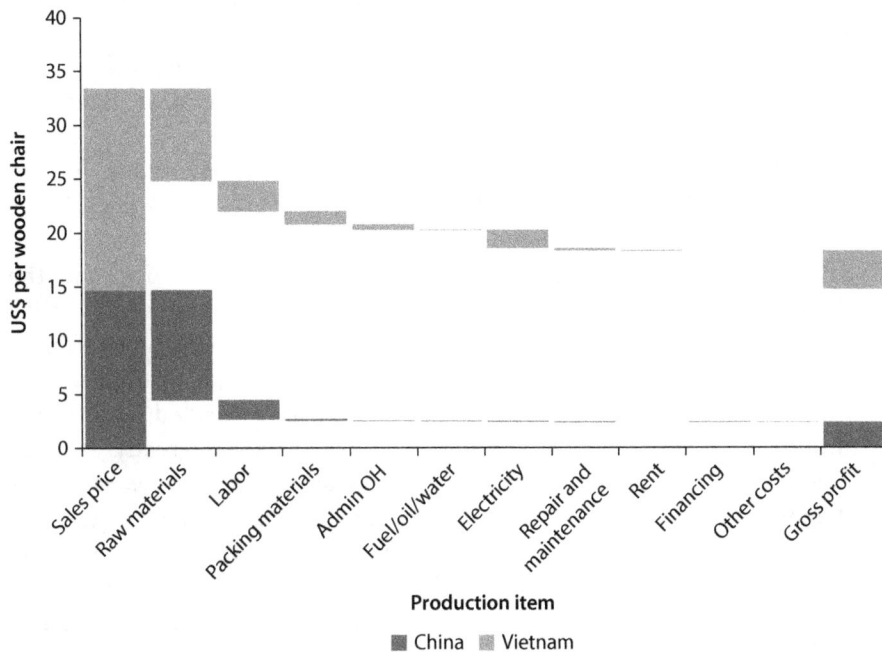

Source: GDS 2011.
Note: Admin OH = administration/overhead.

Our analysis here centers on the production of wooden chairs, but the majority of furniture enterprises in Vietnam do not specialize in only one segment of furniture manufacturing. Furniture enterprises also produce parts or completed furniture pieces directly for foreign furniture suppliers according to the designs of the buyers. Similar to the apparel and leather sectors, producers of wood products do not participate much in product development, and they therefore have skill deficiencies in design, branding, marketing, human resource management, and the sourcing of materials.

Figure 6.2 illustrates the higher cost of a wooden chair in Vietnam arising because of the lower cost of raw materials, but the higher cost of labor and other inputs. The breakdown shows clearly that specific areas in the production process could be addressed to increase efficiency and lower costs. Evaluating the costs of labor, packing materials, and electricity may be an initial step toward reducing the bottlenecks that cause the industry to be less competitive.

The less binding constraints include the following:

- *The rising cost of imported timber and the significant reliance on these imports:* More than 80 percent of the timber used to make wood products in Vietnam is imported. On average, the country imports nearly 3.5 million cubic meters of timber each year. Sawn timber accounts for 65 percent of the imports—at a cost of over $1 billion—and is destined mainly for the processed wood industry.
- *Lack of access to suitable land:* Large-scale investors have difficulty securing land of suitable area and quality. Given that 97.6 percent of the furniture enterprises in Vietnam are small or medium, coupled with the multitude of smallholder tree farms, the development of a plantation-based wood industry at scale is challenging.
- *The expanding regulatory framework related to environmentally friendly methods and the sourcing of wood:* The Forest Stewardship Council issues independent certificates to reflect environmental and social compliance with its standards. Customers in the European Union, Japan, and the United States are increasingly demanding council chain-of-custody certification on wood products they purchase. Additionally, the European Union (Due Diligence Regulation; Forest Law Enforcement, Governance, and Trade) and the United States (the Lacey Act) have enacted laws to ban imports of illegal wood and wood products. This has greatly affected Vietnam, which purchases timber from Cambodia, the Lao People's Democratic Republic, and Myanmar, where traceability and sustainable practices are not strictly enforced. Laws to eliminate formaldehyde in wood products are also being introduced. The Vietnamese wood processing industry has already begun transitioning its sourcing away from natural forest logs to logs cut from trees grown on small plantations. Although more than 2.5 million hectares are estimated to be involved in forest plantation wood production in the country, the Forest Stewardship Council has certified only 10,000 hectares. The areas certified by the council produce mainly short-rotation wood chips rather than sawn logs. Furthermore, many firms are implementing chain-of-custody supply management policies to avoid sanctions and to safeguard their reputations.[4] Almost 200 wood processing firms use chain-of-custody management practices.

Policy Recommendations

The wood products industry requires certain technical and managerial skills that cannot be replaced by cheap, abundant labor. Vietnam has been competitive in the sector, but, to sustain competitiveness over the medium to long term, it must address the issues of productivity and excessive input use, as follows:

- *Implement vocational training to help reduce the shortages in skilled labor and management.* Even the most basic furniture processing and assembly skills appear to be in limited supply. To enhance productivity and efficiency, there needs to be a viable training mechanism for workers and line managers. Training schemes would also help workers develop local design capabilities and more sustainable production and marketing practices. Technical assistance and other training, such as Kaizen methods, would also be beneficial (see chapter 3). Technical training has raised productivity in places such as Phu Khe village, near Hanoi, where carpenters have been trained to use modern techniques to produce furniture made of softwood. If such strategies were adopted sector-wide, this would improve productivity and reduce excesses in the use of inputs, such as glue and varnish. Vietnam could thus lower production costs and become more competitive with China. Measures to address vocational training are discussed further in chapter 9.
- *Develop plug-and-play industrial parks.* These parks would facilitate the access of small and medium enterprises (SMEs) to utilities, land, finance, and skills and could offer technical assistance programs for owner-managers and workers. The parks could also be used to make training more affordable and accessible.
- *Encourage new investment and technology upgrades.* Replacing old equipment and upgrading technology through substantial new investment are critical in all stages of the supply chain. This requires the following:
  - Promote foreign direct investment preferably through joint ventures.
  - Enhance investment in training to add to technical and modern design skills.
  - Build new, integrated wood product clusters close to forested areas.
  - Stimulate private investment in plantation forestry to meet the future demand for fuelwood and for long-term supplies for wood-based industries. Production plantations are still essential for maintaining sustainable forestry resources.
  - Foster greater productivity on sustainable private plantations. The focus should be on site productivity rather than area coverage. New supplies of raw materials could be produced if sites and tree species were properly selected. More aggressive policy initiatives to comply with Forest Stewardship Council certification and rule-of-origin regulations are likely to become necessary for the growth and success of the sector.

Notes

1. The data in this section have been gathered from reports by the International Trade Center based on UN Comtrade (United Nations Commodity Trade Statistics Database), Statistics Division, Department of Economic and Social Affairs, United Nations, New York, http://comtrade.un.org/db/.

2. Our sample of Vietnamese producers sell mostly in foreign markets. For both China and Vietnam, the chairs in the sample are made of pine species wood (20–25 cubic meters of wood per 1,000 chairs). They are constructed of dried wood, finished with varnish or paint, and assembled. They are not upholstered.

3. Wages also reflect this difference. Skilled labor in Vietnam earns $181–$259 a month, and unskilled labor earns only $85–$135 a month.

4. Chain of custody refers to the tracking of certified material from the forest to the final product.

Reference

GDS (Global Development Solutions). 2011. *The Value Chain and Feasibility Analysis; Domestic Resource Cost Analysis.* Vol. 2 of *Light Manufacturing in Africa: Targeted Policies to Enhance Private Investment and Create Jobs.* Washington, DC: World Bank. http://go.worldbank.org/6G2A3TFI20.

CHAPTER 7

Metal Products

Vietnam currently imports 94 percent of its metalworking equipment and mechanical products. Only 6 percent of the country's demand is met by local manufacturers. Yet, labor costs in the metal sector are low; productivity is high; and the demand associated with investment projects is outstripping supply. Production costs are lower in Vietnam than in China. The constraints in the sector include the inadequate domestic supply of inputs, the excessive use of utilities, and significant worker absenteeism in some firms. Policies to address these issues might include increasing the exploitation of iron ore deposits subject to environmental protection; developing plug-and-play industrial parks to facilitate the access of small and medium enterprises (SMEs) to utilities, land, and financing, as well as to improved skills through technical assistance programs for owner-managers and workers; and promoting foreign direct investment (FDI) to make up for the capital shortages.

Description of the Sector

According to the World Steel Association, total global crude steel production in 2008 amounted to 1.3 billion tons.[1] The global export value of items made of iron or steel was $226 billion in 2009. China was the leading exporter that year, at $34 billion (15 percent of global exports) (figure 7.1).

According to the South East Asia Iron and Steel Institute, the total consumption of steel products in Vietnam reached approximately 10.6 million metric tons in 2009, and more than 40 percent of this total was accounted for by imports (SEAISI 2012). By 2015, Vietnam will require an estimated 15 million tons of steel a year. Only 6 percent of the demand for metalworking equipment and mechanical products is satisfied by local manufacturers. Similarly, because industrial production in Vietnam is growing at 19 percent a year, imports of steel products have been increasing at an annual rate of 30 percent. In 2010, the industry met 54 percent of the country's total demand for steel ingots, 40 percent of the demand for cold steel, and 100 percent of the demand for building steel.

Figure 7.1 Leading Exporters of Iron or Steel Products, Worldwide, 2009

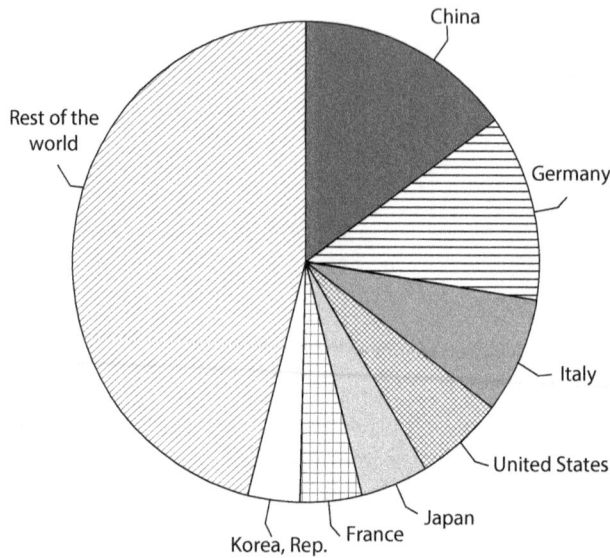

Source: GDS 2011.
Note: The world aggregation represents the sum of reporting and nonreporting countries.

Vietnam is a major importer of low- and medium-grade steel products from Japan and imports even lower-grade steel from China, the Russian Federation, and Ukraine, which suggests that the market for high-grade steel is limited. While the demand for high-grade hot coil and cold rolled sheets for the manufacture of mechanical products, such as motorcycles, is substantial, the demand is restrained for other high-grade products, such as the heavy plates used in large-scale industrial production (in shipbuilding, for instance) and the galvanized steel used in automotive production.

The metals industry in Vietnam employs over 130,000 workers across more than 3,700 enterprises, compared with 3.6 million workers in more than 24,500 firms in China (table 7.1). In both countries, men dominate, representing approximately three-quarters of the workforce.

Our analysis is based on 12 firms in China and 10 firms in Vietnam. We use crown corks (bottle caps) as the reference product.

Tariffs and taxes raise the production prices in Vietnam. The tariff rates (preferential) for the base metals and metal parts relevant to our analysis are around 27 percent (20 percent in China). The common effective preferential tariff covers other products at an average of 2.3 percent. There is also a value added tax of 10 percent (17 percent in China, which is, however, reimbursed), an income tax of 28 percent (25 percent in China), and an export tax that reaches as high as 45 percent. While Vietnamese enterprises enjoy preferential

Table 7.1 The Processed Metal Industry, China and Vietnam, 2009

Indicator	China	Vietnam
Total imports, $, millions	8,920.7	1,548.4
Total exports, $, millions	33,781.1	706.2
Companies, total	24,547	3,762
Small, %	20.0	38.7
Medium, %	50.0	59.3
Large, %	30	2.0
Workers, total (estimate)	3,561,638	130,436
Men, %	73	74
Women, %	27	26

Sources: GDS 2011; UN Comtrade (United Nations Commodity Trade Statistics Database), Statistics Division, Department of Economic and Social Affairs, United Nations, New York, http://comtrade.un.org/db/.

rates for utilities (electricity and water), there are no other subsidies. Similar firms in China enjoy a subsidy of 9 percent for iron sheets and subsidies of 5–13 percent for iron products.

The Potential

Vietnam exported approximately $706 million worth of processed metal products in 2009, while importing more than $1.5 billion worth of such products. This shows that there is an immediate opportunity for the sector to meet the demands of the rapidly growing domestic market. SMEs dominate the market. In crown corks, our survey reveals that, relative to China, Vietnam could become a higher-productivity, lower-cost production location, though the firms in our survey in Vietnam do not appear to be exporting yet. The cost of producing crown corks in Vietnam averages $4.72 per 1,000 pieces (table 7.2). Corks of the same quality cost approximately $5.07 per 1,000 pieces to produce in China. The primary raw material (tin-free steel) accounts for 72 percent of the value chain in Vietnam; in China, where locally available tin-free steel is cheaper, it accounts for only 42 percent. However, the prices are lower in Vietnam.

Factors that could allow Vietnam to develop a competitive domestic metal products industry include the following:

• *Low labor costs:* Similar to the situation in the apparel and leather sectors, the labor costs of skilled metalworkers in Vietnam are less than 22 percent of the corresponding costs in China.
• *High productivity:* Workers in best practice firms produce 25–27 pieces a day in Vietnam, but only 13–25 pieces a day in China.
• *Many metal products are heavy and bulky:* The low value-to-weight ratio typical of metal products makes local or regional imports preferable. This is especially important because China imports such large quantities.

Table 7.2 Benchmarking Key Production Variables, Crown Corks, China and Vietnam, 2010

Indicator	China	Vietnam
Factory		
Capacity utilization, %	95–100	70–100
Installed capacity, pieces per day, 1,000s	427–2,500	800–8,000
Labor absenteeism rate, %	1–2	0–5
Average monthly salary or wage		
Skilled, $	265–369	168–233
Unskilled, $	192–265	117–142
Days of operation per month	26–28	26–30
Average age of major equipment, years	4.5–5.3	1.3–1.8
Exported output, finished primary product		
Direct export without consolidators or brokers, %	0	0
Indirect export through local consolidators, %	20–60	0
Indirect export through overseas consolidators, %	0	0
Domestically sold output, finished primary product		
Direct sales to wholesalers or retailers without consolidators, %	0	100
Direct sales through own outlets, shops, or showrooms, %	40–100	0
Indirect sales through local consolidators or traders, %	0	0
Unit production cost, $ per 1,000 pieces	4.81–5.32	4.43–5.01
Average selling price, $ per 1,000 pieces		
Factory gate	5.75–6.64	5.31–5.80
Wholesale	5.90–7.08	n.a.
Free on board	6.19–7.08	n.a.

Source: GDS 2011.
Note: n.a. = not applicable.

- *The demand associated with investment projects is outstripping supply:* According to the Ministry of Industry and Trade, as many as 65 steel projects (7 FDI projects and 58 domestic and joint venture projects) are in the pipeline, and these represent an aggregate yearly capacity of more than 100,000 tons spread across 30 provinces in the country. Because of this surge in activity, the ministry has asked cities and provinces to stop granting new investment licenses for steel projects and to revise existing contracts.

The distribution of resources across the value chain is somewhat similar in both countries. If we exclude primary raw materials, the seal making and sealing stage of crown cork production accounts for 14–30 percent of the value chain, of which more than 78 percent is comprised of consumables, such as polyvinyl chloride compound and bonding chemicals. Coating and printing represent the third-largest segment of the value chain among enterprises in China, accounting for 9.0–17.0 percent, compared with about 5.4 percent in Vietnam.

The Main Constraints on Competitiveness

Despite higher steel prices, the manufacturing costs of metal products are lower in Vietnam than in China. However, as in the apparel and leather sectors, the lower production costs arise because of the lower wage rates, which will not always be available. Certain issues must be addressed to maintain long-term competitiveness, as follows:

- *The inadequate domestic supply* of inputs is the main driver of the high price of imported steel in Vietnam. The high prices of the raw materials and the steel products make Vietnam's steel industry vulnerable to price fluctuations on the world market. As the country integrates more fully in the global economy, the steel industry needs to address this high import dependence to compete in the more open economic environment. The most daunting challenge facing the Vietnamese steel industry is access to and the price of raw materials.

- *Excessive utility use* is characteristic of this sector despite fairly new equipment. In China, crown cork manufacturing firms spend $8 on utilities per million pieces produced; the corresponding amount in Vietnam is $70. In addition, Vietnamese firms spend 250 times more than Chinese firms on the water needed to produce the same quantity and quality of crown corks. Vietnamese enterprises use 1,115–1,633 kilowatt hours of electricity per million pieces, but Chinese enterprises use only 37–80 kilowatt hours per million. The fuel consumption rate of a factory in Vietnam is more than 40 times that of a factory in China. All these factors add up to higher-than-necessary production costs in Vietnam that nearly wipe out the advantage that low labor costs provide.

- *Significant worker absenteeism* is an issue in some Vietnamese firms in the sector (up to 5 percent, as opposed to 2 percent in China). Perhaps more noteworthy, while labor costs in Vietnam are competitive, the labor cost differential between China and Vietnam, particularly relative to skilled workers, is substantially narrower than the gap found in other, less technical sectors such as apparel, where the cost of skilled labor in Vietnam is less than one-third that in China.

Policy Recommendations

To remain competitive in the long run and to exploit fully Vietnam's potential in this sector, the government should consider the following measures:

- *Promote the exploitation of the country's iron ore deposits* subject to environmental protection and conduct an in-depth feasibility study to assess the potential competitiveness of the domestic steel industry. The export of iron ore affects domestic steel manufacturing enterprises to the extent that they face shortages in raw materials and are forced to import these raw materials at substantial cost. (Steel is a low value-to-weight item and is subject to import tariffs of 27 percent.) According to Vietnam Steel Association estimates, the country has combined deposits of more than 1.2 billion tons of iron ore. The largest mines are in Thach Khe, in central Ha Tinh Province, where there is a deposit of more than 544 million tons, and Quy Xa, in northern Lao Cai Province, where there is an estimated deposit of 112 million tons. The untapped iron ore deposits could substantially reduce the production costs associated with imported steel. More exploration of iron ore and coal deposits while taking proper measures to protect the environment could enhance the competitiveness of the steel industry in the world market.

• *Develop plug-and-play industrial parks* to facilitate the access of SMEs to land and financing, as well as to skills through technical assistance programs for owner-managers and workers. This would help especially in identifying ways to reduce the overuse of utilities.

• *Promote FDI to make up for capital shortages.* Local industry has been able to build only one production chain to produce steel ingots from iron ore. Most of Vietnam's iron ore must therefore be sold abroad unprocessed. Attracting foreign capital is essential for larger projects in the steel industry. In addition, the transfer of technologies and managerial skills from foreign enterprises will be critical for the development of Vietnamese steel technology.

Note

1. "Annual Crude Steel Production, 2000–2009," World Steel Association, Brussels (accessed March 23, 2013), http://www.worldsteel.org/dms/internetDocumentList /statistics-archive/production-archive/steel-archive/steel-annually/Annual-steel -2000-2009/document/Annual%20steel%202000-2009.pdf.

References

GDS (Global Development Solutions). 2011. *The Value Chain and Feasibility Analysis; Domestic Resource Cost Analysis.* Vol. 2 of *Light Manufacturing in Africa: Targeted Policies to Enhance Private Investment and Create Jobs.* Washington, DC: World Bank. http://go.worldbank.org/6G2A3TFI20.

SEAISI (South East Asia Iron and Steel Institute). 2012. *2012 Steel Statistical Yearbook.* Selangor, Malaysia: SEAISI. http://www.seaisi.org/html/yearbook_publication.asp.

CHAPTER 8

Agribusiness

Vietnam has significant potential in agribusiness in domestic and export markets. However, unlike the apparel and leather sectors, the agribusiness sector lags far behind regional competitors. The main reasons for this deficient performance include the poor quality of inputs and low labor productivity. The key challenges in the agricultural input and output markets are the limitations in commercial farming, the weak financial capacity of the many small companies, the lack of access to information among producers, the absence of agro-processing clusters, poor sanitary conditions, poor packaging, and the need for the greater availability and use of veterinary care. To address the problems and constraints, commercial farming should be facilitated; contract farming should be encouraged; clusters should be formed more quickly; training services for food production under hygienic conditions should be enhanced; the packaging industry should be promoted; and sectoral associations should be strengthened.

Description of the Sector

Agriculture is the mainstay of the Vietnamese economy. Rice is the principal crop and is grown over a large portion of the cultivable land in the country. Other crops include sweet potatoes, sorghum, corn, cassava, fruits, vegetables, and beans. Of the total land in northern Vietnam, only 15 percent is suitable for cultivation, of which nearly 14 percent has been cultivated intensively. As demonstrated by the success of the rice and coffee industries, Vietnam has substantial potential in agribusiness in domestic and export markets.

In the world market, China has become a major player in the agribusiness sector, with total production exceeding a value of $990 billion. In both China and Vietnam, the sector is dominated by small and medium enterprises (SMEs) (94 percent in Vietnam and over 75 percent in China), and there are relatively few large companies. In Vietnam, the sector employs fewer than 500,000 workers, compared with nearly 10 million in China (table 8.1).

Table 8.1 The Agribusiness Sector, China and Vietnam, 2010

Indicator	China	Vietnam
Total imports, $, 1,000s	6,596	25,360
Total exports, $, 1,000s	96,003	15,848
Companies, total	12,903	5,979
Small, %	35.0	45.4
Medium, %	40.0	48.7
Large, %	25.0	5.9
Workforce		
Total (estimate)	9,956,316	451,360
Share of total labor force, %	1.2	1.0
Men, %	73	45
Women, %	27	55

Sources: GDS 2011; UN Comtrade (United Nations Commodity Trade Statistics Database), Statistics Division, Department of Economic and Social Affairs, United Nations, New York, http://comtrade.un.org/db/.

The industry needs to address several important issues to achieve greater, more sustainable productivity in the context of the trend toward more liberalization and deeper trade integration. Unlike the apparel and leather sectors, agribusiness in Vietnam lags far behind regional competitors. The main reasons for this poor performance include low productivity, the low quality of inputs, high costs, and especially, the weakness of processing industries. These are huge challenges for the country's agribusiness producers.

Wheat Milling

Agribusiness is a broad sector with numerous branches and many products within each branch.

In wheat flour, Turkey was the top exporter in 2009, at $581 million in export value. China exported $96 million in wheat flour (figure 8.1).

The cost of milling wheat in Vietnam was $359–$463 per ton in 2010, which is close to or above the cost in China ($322–$377). The main reason for the difference is the price of wheat, the type of wheat used (hard versus soft), the period when the wheat is sourced (because prices fluctuate widely in local and international markets), and the origin and mix of the wheat used (local versus imported). Because wheat accounts for more than 80 percent of the cost of wheat flour, the higher price of the wheat explains most of the higher wheat flour production costs in Vietnam. The price of domestic wheat is 40 percent higher in Vietnam than in China (table 8.2). Our analysis of wheat is based on 10 firms in China and 9 firms in Vietnam.

The reference year in our analysis, 2010, was exceptional in world wheat markets. Because of weather conditions, mainly in the Russian Federation (and, to a degree, in Canada), wheat prices in international markets soared more than 40 percent between July and August, the highest monthly increase in more than 50 years. International wheat prices continued to shift later in 2010, albeit the rate of change was not as high as the July–August spike. The variations in the

Figure 8.1 Leading Exporters of Wheat or Meslin Flour Products, Worldwide, 2009

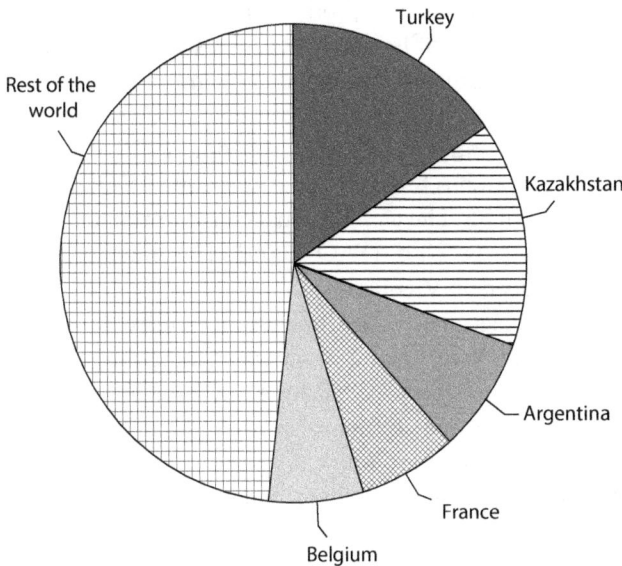

Source: GDS 2011.
Note: The world aggregation represents the sum of reporting and nonreporting countries. Meslin is mixed grain, especially rye mixed with wheat.

Table 8.2 Raw Material Input Comparison, Wheat Flour, China and Vietnam, 2010

	China		Vietnam	
Indicator	Total cost	% of total input	Total cost	% of total input
Raw materials, per ton of wheat flour	$322	n.a.	$323	n.a.
Domestic wheat, per ton	$192	60.0	$269	73.7
Imported wheat, per ton	none	none	$208	n.a.
Raw material inputs, % of value chain	85	n.a.	81	n.a.

Source: GDS 2011.
Note: n.a. = not applicable.

prices of the raw materials (wheat) presented in this analysis should thus be considered in the context of this extreme price volatility during 2010.

In both China and Vietnam, agribusiness is the focus of a wide array of tariffs. In China, there are more than 722 tariffs in the sector, and the average rate is 15 percent. In Vietnam, there are more than 40,773 tariff lines in the fast and normal tracks of the common effective preferential tariff scheme, which, at an average rate, has been as low as 2.3 percent. China has a relatively high tax rate, ranging from 10 percent for fish to 20 percent for maize, as well as a value added tax of 17 percent. In Vietnam, the average value added tax is 10 percent. Although there are a range of taxes and levies imposed on agribusiness in China, there are also tax refunds that run from 8 percent for rice to 15 percent for maize; the average tax refund is 16 percent. Producers in Vietnam do not enjoy such refunds.

Light Manufacturing in Vietnam • http://dx.doi.org/10.1596/978-1-4648-0034-4

Dairy Products

The demand for milk is increasing in Vietnam, but there is a wide gap between this demand and the nation's milk production capacity. Vietnam still has to import around three-quarters of its dairy needs. This is partly because milk production per cow in Vietnam lags behind that in more industrialized nations. The approximately 115,000 cows in Vietnam yield 280,000 tons of milk a year. The population of the country was 86 million people in 2010. Vietnam's yearly per capita milk consumption is thus estimated at around 15 kilograms, compared with the Asian average of 35. The global annual consumption of milk was around 82.1 kilograms a person in 2005 (FAO 2009). This highlights the potential market for dairy producers in Vietnam.

In Vietnam, the average dairy farm operation profiled in our analysis was medium in size and had fewer than 200 animals (table 8.3). This differs from China, where the dairy farms profiled for our study have hundreds of cows. This difference is evident in indicators of the value of production, exports, number of firms, number of employees, and so on.

The cost of producing milk in Vietnam ranges from $0.15 to $0.29 a liter (table 8.4). This is competitive with production in China, where the cost ranges from $0.23 to $0.28. Perhaps the most notable difference between the two countries is the average yield per milking cow. With proper animal husbandry, cows in China produce at a rate of 20 liters per cow per day, while, in Vietnam, the yield rates generally range from 4.2 to 15.9 liters.

Globally, dairy products worth $51 billion were exported in 2009. Germany, France, the Netherlands, and New Zealand were the leading exporters, at more than $5 billion each (figure 8.2). China is a major producer of dairy products, and the country is facing a rapid shift in dietary habits, especially among urban consumers. This shift is reflected in steady growth in the dairy industry, which now produces dairy products worth more than $29 billion. The number of consumers of these products is expected to increase 50 percent over the next seven years, and overall global demand for

Table 8.3 The Dairy Industry, China and Vietnam, 2010

Indicator	China	Vietnam
Production, total value, $	29,450,322,733	530,225,356
Imports, total value, $	892,667,190	539,780,000
Exports, total value, $	51,402,368	156,700,000
Companies, total	12,903	1,670
Small, %	35.0	43.4
Medium, %	40.0	55.1
Large, %	25.0	1.5
Workers, total (estimate)	9,956,316	54,794
Men, %	73.0	75.5
Women, %	27.0	24.5

Source: GDS 2011.

Table 8.4 Average Cost of Milk Production, Selected Countries, 2010

US$ per liter

Economy	Average cost
New Zealand	0.13
Australia	0.16
India	0.19
Vietnam	0.22
China	0.25
United States	0.27
European Union	0.29
Tanzania	0.42
Ethiopia	0.47
Zambia	0.52

Source: GDS 2011.

Figure 8.2 Leading Exporters, Dairy Products, Worldwide, 2009

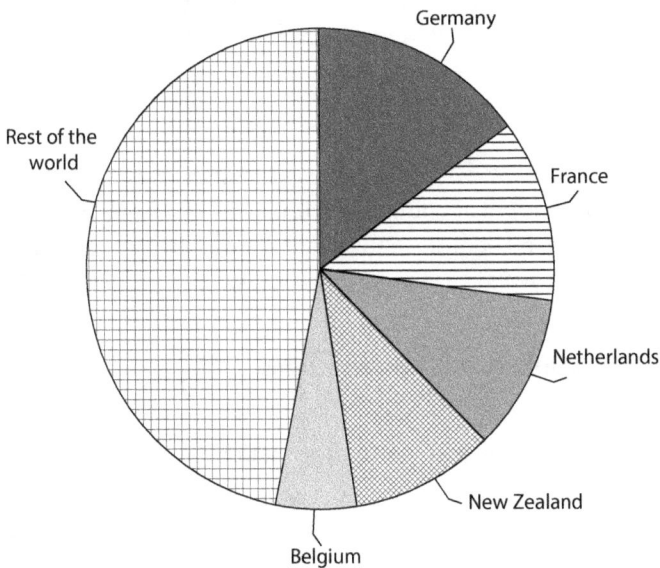

Source: GDS 2011.
Note: The world aggregation represents the sum of reporting and nonreporting countries.

dairy products in developing countries is expected to rise about 1.2 percent each year (FAO 2009). This surging demand is opening the door to an expansion in exports.

According to the Ministry of Industry and Trade, despite substantial growth in agribusiness, Vietnam continues to import significant amounts of food and farm products. Its main sources of the imports of these products are India (16 percent), the United States (13 percent), and China (11 percent). Under the Association of Southeast Asian Nations–China Free Trade Agreement and the common effective preferential tariff, the commitments among the association countries have led to less expensive imports; import tariffs are 0–5 percent. These results are favorable for consumers. Nonetheless, there is a concern that the country will need to reduce its reliance on imported food and agricultural products through the more stringent application of technical and quality specifications.

The Potential

Wheat Milling

The potential of the wheat milling industry in Vietnam stems from the following:

- Because of low wages, the cost to mill wheat (excluding the cost of the wheat) is half as much in Vietnam relative to China. Skilled and unskilled labor wages are, on average, one and half times lower in Vietnam.
- The climatic and soil conditions are good in some areas.
- Domestic demand is rising, and Vietnam's access to the global market is widening.

Dairy Products

The labor productivity rate in dairy farming in Vietnam is low, at 2.5–3.9 liters of output per person per day, compared with 23.5–53.1 liters per person per day in China. In addition, most of the equipment used in dairy farming is much older in Vietnam (5.5–8.0 years) than in China (2.5–4.0 years) (table 8.5).

The Main Constraints on Competitiveness

Wheat Milling

Vietnam faces several challenges in the production of wheat:

- Shortages of high-yielding seeds and agricultural inputs
- Lack of irrigated farming
- Entry barriers for large commercial farms, including land policy issues
- Lack of appropriate storage infrastructure
- Absence of market mechanisms to encourage stable, predictable prices
- Lack of working capital among wholesalers

The distribution of costs along the value chain differs in China and Vietnam. In China, handling and storage, as well as transport and delivery (to the buyer), account for nearly 10 percent of the value chain. In Vietnam, however, milling and packing account for nearly 10 percent of the value chain, while administrative overhead accounts for 6 percent (figure 8.3).

Several key factors affect the competitiveness of the milling subsector, particularly wheat milling. Thus, in Vietnam, the mills tend to be large, centralized

Table 8.5 Benchmarking Key Production Variables, Dairy Farming, China and Vietnam, 2010

Indicator	China	Vietnam
Factory		
Male-to-female worker ratio	6.5–52.3	—
Average yield rate per milking day, liters per cow	20.0–20.5	4.2–15.9
Labor absenteeism rate, %	—	0–1
Average monthly salary or wage		
Skilled, $	177–206	—
Unskilled, $	118–133	31–78
Days of operation per month	30	21–30
Average age of major equipment, years	2.5–4.0	5.5–8.0
Exported output, finished primary product, %		
Direct export without consolidators or brokers	0	0
Indirect export through local consolidators	0	0
Indirect export through overseas consolidators	0	0
Domestically sold output, finished primary product		
Direct sales to wholesalers and retailers without consolidators, %	100	0–100
Direct sales through own outlets, shops, or showrooms, %	0	0–100
Indirect sales through local consolidators or traders, %	0	0
Unit production cost, $ per liter	0.23–0.28	0.08–0.29
Average selling price, $		
Factory gate	0.27–0.32	0.38–0.39
Wholesale	0.27–0.32	0.36–0.37

Source: GDS 2011.
Note: — = not available.

(installed output capacity of 21–700 tons a day), and underused; in China, the mills tend to be smaller (installed output capacity of 15–30 tons a day), decentralized, and located closer to the source of wheat production. Partly as a consequence of the operation of large centralized mills, capacity use in Vietnam is as low as 80 percent in some mills; in China, capacity use is 95–100 percent.

The cost of raw materials (the wheat) generally makes up the largest share of the wheat milling value chain. Raw material inputs account for 85 percent of the overall value chain in China, while, in Vietnam, wheat accounts for 81 percent of the value chain (see table 8.2). However, in Vietnam, the price of imported wheat is lower (by as much as 29 percent) than the price of the wheat produced locally, raising concerns about the efficiency of Vietnam's farming operations and about the differences between the two countries in the incentive structures that affect the cost of agricultural inputs.

Because various parts of Vietnam are characterized by different opportunities and constraints, farmers face unique challenges depending on the region and the crop. The main constraint is the high cost of agricultural inputs. The average cost of wheat processing per ton—excluding the cost of wheat grain and

Figure 8.3 Cost of Key Production and Margin Items, Wheat, China and Vietnam, 2010

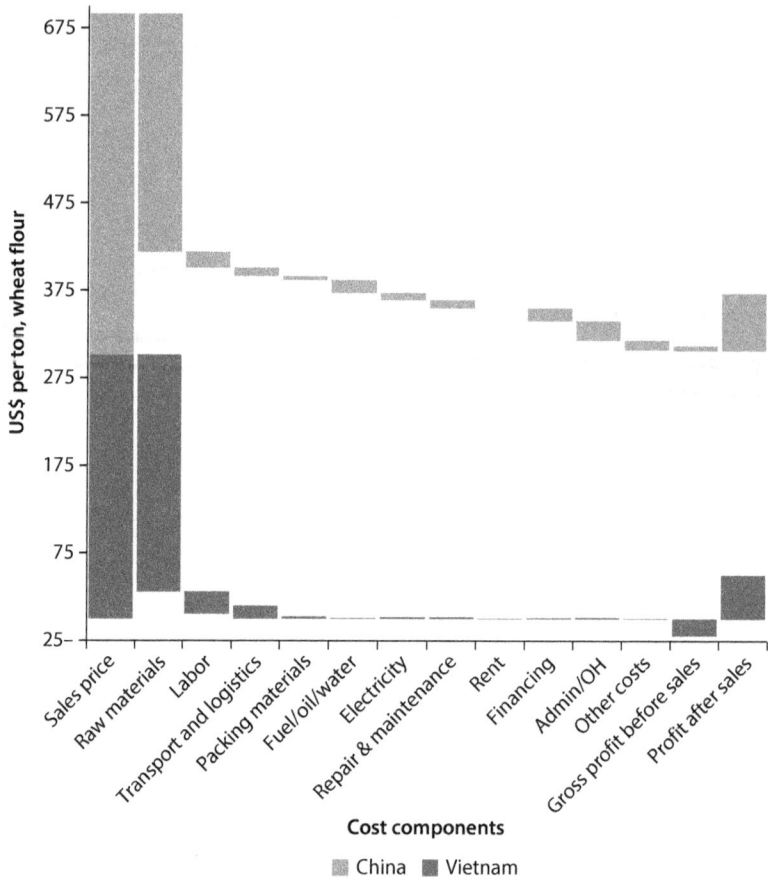

Source: GDS 2011.
Note: Admin/OH = administration/overhead.

packaging—is $89.49, about 62 percent more expensive than in China. This is reflected in the total production cost, as well as in the selling price. Despite low labor costs, total production costs per ton in Vietnam reach as high as $463, compared with $377 in China, implying that wheat grain prices are high in Vietnam. Consequently, the average selling price of wheat flour is 53 percent higher in Vietnam than in China. Vietnam's yield rate is about 4 tons a hectare, while China's can reach 6 tons a hectare.

The cost of producing wheat flour, including the processing costs for other by-products, ranges from $359 to $463 a ton in Vietnam, an average of 18 percent higher than the cost in China, where the cost ranges from $322 to $377 a ton. Perhaps the most surprising labor-related benchmark is the relatively high labor absenteeism rate reported at mills in Vietnam (3–14 percent). In China, the absenteeism rate is only 1–5 percent.

The ability to process and sell wheat by-products such as bran and germ, in addition to the wheat flour, is vital in the overall economics of a mill. Wheat flour production costs are higher than the average selling price of wheat flour. For this reason, millers recuperate a significant portion of milling costs by processing and selling by-products. In our analysis, the selling price of flour therefore does not include the proceeds from sales of bran and other by-products. In both China and Vietnam, by-products are highly valued thanks to a well-developed value added food processing and animal feed industry. Millers are able to fetch $230–$259 a ton for bran, the most abundant by-product of wheat milling.

In China, wheat flour sells for roughly 30 percent more than wheat; in Vietnam, the corresponding price difference is nearly 40 percent. Vietnamese flour prices are noncompetitive not only because the wheat prices are higher, but also because local millers pass on a large share of the already pricy wheat to the price of flour because of their inability to obtain favorable prices for bran and other wheat by-products.

Fuel and oil use is also significant in Vietnam, ranging from 0.02 to 1.11 liters per ton of milled wheat, which is 28 percent higher than the use rate in China. The milling equipment used in Vietnam requires about twice as much electricity as the milling equipment used in China. This is much more modest than the enormously excessive use of electricity in other areas of light manufacturing production in Vietnam. Indeed, because of the lower utility prices in Vietnam, electricity bills among millers in China and Vietnam are comparable.

Because of the high cost of milling in Vietnam and despite the lower cost of labor there, the average wheat processing costs in Vietnam, excluding the cost of wheat grain and packaging, is $89 a ton, 62 percent higher than the cost in China ($55 a ton).

Meanwhile, in Vietnam, unmilled wheat flour is less expensive and exhibits lower rejection rates. If the costs involved in milling can be reduced, then it will surely be possible to improve the country's competitiveness relative to China.

Dairy Products

Dairy cattle production represents a new farming system in Vietnam. Dairy farmers thus lack knowledge of the management practices they require to obtain a profitable and sustainable level of production. In addition to the price of milk, production costs are important for the economic viability of a dairy farm. The most significant input costs are feed (30–70 percent of expenses) and the purchase of animals (figure 8.4). The lack of knowledge about animal husbandry and veterinary care has also hindered the development of an economically sustainable dairy industry, given that disease and poor practices can greatly diminish the financial returns on a small dairy operation. While labor costs are low per unit in Vietnam, total labor costs are higher because of the lower productivity.

Unlike other subsectors, the cost of electricity in dairy production is higher among Vietnamese firms ($6.87–$9.14 per 1,000 liters) than among Chinese firms ($0.67–$0.78 per 1,000 liters). This suggests that the milk plants surveyed in Vietnam are household businesses and are therefore

Figure 8.4 Cost of Key Production and Margin Items, Dairy Farming, China and Vietnam, 2010

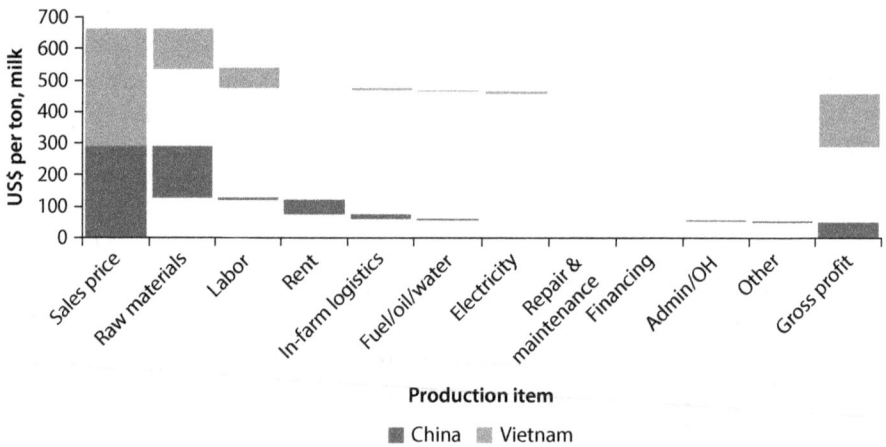

Source: GDS 2011.

charged for electricity at a higher rate than firms in other light manufacturing industries. Electricity use in Vietnamese firms is also much greater, as in all other light manufacturing subsectors. While Vietnamese firms use 126–221 kilowatt hours to produce 1,000 liters of milk, Chinese firms use only 4.92–5.26 kilowatt hours.

Key Challenges in Agribusiness

Key challenges in the agricultural input and output markets in Vietnam include the following:

- The *limited scale of commercial farming* means that agricultural producers are often small and disperse. They have no shared strategy on production procedures or the use of high-yielding seeds, and this leads to difficulties in reaching agreements on product trademarks, quality, and prices. These are the main factors behind the relatively low wheat yield per hectare, which is 4 tons in Vietnam compared with 6 tons in China. There is a need for large-scale farms that raise cows and produce a stable volume of milk to supply processing factories. However, the country lacks large areas of grass to feed cattle. Even if the market is growing, it is not easy for dairy firms to increase their capacity if they depend only on local suppliers for raw materials. The introduction of modern farming techniques is difficult in a smallholder system. Limited access to land is a major constraint on the establishment of larger commercial farms.

- The small companies also have *weak financial capacity*, which is reflected in a shortage of capital to improve production technology and to raise labor productivity. In Vietnam, only 6 percent of agribusiness enterprises are large scale, compared with 25 percent in China (table 8.1).

- The *poor quality of inputs* is a constraining factor among the companies involved in processing agricultural products. The lack of good-quality inputs means the companies are also less competitive in the global market, and they are forced to compete primarily on price.

- Producers have *limited access to information* on modern science and technology and poor awareness of the global market. In countries with a developed agricultural sector, agricultural production is generally conducted by large firms, which can cut production costs by applying advanced production and harvesting technologies.

- The *low agricultural productivity and limited technology* are constraints because Vietnam feeds so many people (86 million) on the output of a relatively small amount of land suitable for agriculture. The country needs to use higher-productivity, higher-technology agriculture to meet its increasing food needs. Relative to developed economies, Vietnam's agricultural sector has been more limited in the use of high-productivity, high-technology agriculture.

- The *supply chain is broken*. Vietnam exports most of its agricultural products without processing. The country has large trade deficits in some agroprocessing industries, such as dairy products and edible oil. This means that there is a significant loss of foreign exchange, as well as the loss of potential employment and value addition.

- There are *few agroprocessing clusters*. Cluster formation is a superior means to address a number of constraints, including limited access to land, poor infrastructure, and cumbersome regulatory procedures and enforcement (see chapter 3). There are only a few agroprocessing clusters in Vietnam.

- *Sanitary conditions are poor, and the regulatory framework is cumbersome.* A large share of food products are produced by small producers in homes and backyards under poor sanitary conditions. Training services in food safety are inadequate, and the infrastructure for standards and management is weak. This burdens companies with costly, time-consuming licensing and inspection procedures in food production, distribution, import, and export.

- *Good-quality, affordable packaging materials are lacking.* Good-quality packaging at competitive prices with appropriate labeling is essential for the effective marketing of agroprocessing products. Appropriate packaging includes metal cans, plastic bottles, shrink wrap in plastic bags, and glass jars with metal closures. Small companies lack access to these forms of packaging. The government should introduce and support the use of bar codes.

- There is a *need for the greater availability and use of veterinary care*. Farmers should be provided with more education and training, and animals should be more well cared for. Focusing investment resources on improving productivity and building skills and knowledge would be beneficial for overall competitiveness.

Policy Recommendations

The following measures are recommended:

- *Facilitate commercial farming.* Establishing commercial farming in designated areas would contribute to competitiveness. Nucleus farm hubs and an outgrower scheme might include nucleus commercial farms with storage and processing facilities that are connected to nearby villages over feeder roads, as well as to power and water services. Such an initiative would require strong public-private partnerships to build the necessary infrastructure and arrange services, such as the leasing of farm machinery and equipment.

- *Encourage contract farming.* This is an option for addressing the lack of access by small farmers to agricultural inputs and services and for formalizing the relationship between smallholders and the agroprocessing industry. This arrangement should be implemented as a pilot project, and if the pilot project succeeds, wider adoption should be encouraged.

- *Speed up cluster formation.* The successful formation of clusters requires collaboration among major stakeholders, such as local governments and industry associations, in building the necessary infrastructure, establishing effective supply chain management, creating training-with-production services, and developing market links. A pilot approach would be appropriate in cluster formation.

- *Enhance the training services in food production under hygienic conditions.* Training initiatives for small agroprocessing companies already exist. A noteworthy initiative is the planned establishment of training in food processing and food processing production centers, such as those financed in Tanzania by the Korea International Cooperation Agency. Similar programs should be developed under donor-financed technical assistance organized by industry associations. Training can also be conducted through clusters.

- *Encourage the packaging industry.* An assessment should be carried out to identify the packaging needs of the agroprocessing industry, and a feasibility study should be conducted on an investment scheme in the production of packaging materials. Once this work is completed, the government should seek foreign direct investment in this important area, preferably in partnership with local entrepreneurs.

- *Strengthen industry associations.* Industry associations provide critical services to members, such as advocacy, policy dialogue, technical assistance, training on skills and standards, and market information. The government should encourage the formation of these associations and facilitate their growth.

References

FAO (Food and Agriculture Organization of the United Nations). 2009. *The State of Food and Agriculture 2009: Livestock in the Balance.* Rome: FAO. http://www.fao.org /docrep/012/i0680e/i0680e.pdf.

GDS (Global Development Solutions). 2011. *The Value Chain and Feasibility Analysis; Domestic Resource Cost Analysis.* Vol. 2 of *Light Manufacturing in Africa: Targeted Policies to Enhance Private Investment and Create Jobs.* Washington, DC: World Bank. http://go.worldbank.org/6G2A3TFI20.

CHAPTER 9

Synthesis, Reforms, and Policy Implementation

In this chapter, we first present a synthesis of our findings across the five sectors. We then discuss the implementation of reforms and our policy recommendations.

Vietnam's Potential in Light Manufacturing

There is great potential for the expansion of light manufacturing in Vietnam based on the following:

- Lower wages than China and other emerging economies in certain sectors, as well as a large workforce keen to learn
- Relatively cheap utilities
- Varied climate and soil conditions, which are especially favorable for agribusiness and leather products
- Membership in the Association of Southeast Asian Nations, the Trans-Pacific Partnership (TPP), and the World Trade Organization that provides access to new markets and foreign investment
- A growing domestic market serving more than 85 million people

In the near term, the focus in all five sectors should be primarily on improving productivity and efficiency. Opportunities to create a more integrated value chain would be a medium-term objective. As upgrading occurs, Vietnam will increase its competitiveness in relation to China and will be able to capture greater value added.

The Main Constraints on Competitiveness

The most binding constraints on Vietnam's competitiveness in light manufacturing vary by sector. In the apparel, leather, and wood industries, the shortage in worker skills and the reliance on the methods of cut, make, and trim (CMT) in the case of apparel and leather goods weaken the country's ability to move up the value chain. In metal and agribusiness, the binding constraint appears to be the input industries: producers must rely on external sources and are therefore subject to the vagaries of price instability. In agribusiness, the lack of adequate worker training is also an important constraint. These findings confirm our findings on other countries and have led us to propose a fresh approach to industrialization in developing countries (Dinh and others 2012). Because the most important constraints vary by industry and firm size and are often specific to a sector, effective public policies should be centered on identifying sector-specific constraints and combining market-based measures and targeted government interventions to remove the constraints. This approach builds on the work of Chenery (1979) and Hausmann, Rodrik, and Velasco (2005), who visualize development as a continuous process of specifying binding constraints that limit growth, formulating and implementing policies to relax the constraints, securing modest improvements in performance, and then renewing growth by identifying and pushing against the factors limiting expansion in the new environment. This approach is much more effective than the traditional approach based on economy-wide policy measures, which, because of limited financial and human resources or rent-seeking activities, are typically adopted and then abandoned halfway.

Table 9.1 shows the most important constraints in each sector. It also distinguishes between small and medium enterprises (SMEs) and large enterprises.

Our detailed sector-level diagnostics and our country comparison with China have enabled us to formulate policy recommendations that are specific to each of the light manufacturing sectors and that depend on the sector and on the type and the size of firms. Across the board, the recommendations highlight Vietnam's dependence on imported inputs and the lack of worker and management skills as well as of initiative (for example, the lack of local brands). The next section discusses issues related to labor skills.

Table 9.1 Constraints in Light Manufacturing by Importance, Firm Size, and Sector, Vietnam

Sector	Firm size	Input industries	Land	Finance	Entrepreneurial skills	Worker skills	Trade logistics
Apparel	Smaller	Important	Important	Important	Important	Critical	Important
	Large	Important				Critical	Important
Leather products	Smaller	Important	Important		Critical	Critical	
	Large	Important	Important		Critical	Critical	
Wood products	Smaller	Important			Critical	Critical	Important
	Large	Important	Important		Critical	Critical	Important
Metal products	Smaller	Critical		Important		Important	
	Large	Critical		Important		Important	
Agribusiness	Smaller	Critical	Important	Critical	Important	Important	
	Large	Critical	Critical	Important	Important	Important	

Note: Blank cells indicate that the constraint is not a priority.

Institutional Constraints on Labor Skills[1]

Worker skills are a critical constraint on Vietnam's overall economic success and sustainability, particularly in light manufacturing (see table 9.1). Much of the expertise that light manufacturing requires is obtained through vocational training, which aims to provide practical skills to students. Because it is closely connected to production, vocational training contributes directly to labor and economic restructuring, making this type of education especially relevant to economic growth.

Labor Skills and Vocational Training

According to the Ministry of Labor, Invalids, and Social Affairs (MOLISA), Vietnam's labor force totaled 47.7 million in 2009, and the labor market must absorb around 1.6 million new entrants each year. Labor force participation, at 75.6 percent, is relatively high in Vietnam, and the highest rates are among the prime age-group of 25–54 years (MOLISA 2011). The main income-generating asset of many Vietnamese is labor, and participation in the labor market is usually crucial for survival and development. The quality of labor is therefore critical. Of particular concern is the low technical and professional educational attainment among the workforce. Of the population aged 15 years and older, only 4.4 percent hold a tertiary degree, and 8.9 percent have attended some kind of technical school, while 86.7 percent are unskilled.

A recent survey of 76 manufacturers involved in the production of electronics, motorcycles and other automotive products, as well as in other mechanical sectors, reveals that, while graduates in technical vocational education and training (TVET) are good at maintaining company rules and operational standards, they do not possess good production-site management skills (Mori, Hoang, and Thuy 2010). In addition, they do not actively improve operations using specific techniques, make their workplaces clean and efficient, or work well as part of a team. Furthermore, while these graduates are able to learn to use new machinery quickly, more specific technical skills (plastic mold injection, casting, and forging) and basic engineering knowledge (blueprint reading) are lacking.

Key Players

Two key players in worker skill training are MOLISA and the Ministry of Education and Training (MOET). What may be called formal TVET includes various secondary education programs administered by MOET or by the General Department of Vocational Training (GDVT) within MOLISA. The GDVT is responsible for 871 TVET institutions (40 vocational colleges, 232 secondary vocational schools, and 599 vocational training centers). MOET manages around 272 technical secondary schools and 228 colleges and universities.

Under the Law on Vocational Training, there are three levels of training: primary, which includes short-term vocational training and retraining programs; intermediate, which is for students who have completed lower or upper secondary education and which consists of programs ranging from one to three years; and college level, which combines general education subjects and specific occupational subjects and leads to a diploma and the ability to enroll in a higher education degree program. There are various forms of vocational training, including full-time training at vocational schools and at businesses, part-time training, and training schemes set up by other ministries, enterprises in industrial zones, and traditional handicraft villages.

Enrollment in the formal system has grown substantially in recent years. In 2001–09, the number of students in the GDVT-administered system doubled, from 526,000 to 1.34 million, more than a million of whom were students in short courses. The 272 technical secondary schools and 228 colleges managed by MOET were also delivering TVET programs among some 550,000 students.

The TVET environment includes more than 800 other providers offering short-term training courses (for example, employment service offices). Formal apprenticeship training exists, but is infrequently implemented. Another important mode of training is informal training, mainly on the job, which is not formally recognized.

Training institutions are owned and financed by a variety of actors, including provincial and district governments, central ministries, mass organizations, trade unions, companies, and private institutions. Around 30 percent of the institutions under the GDVT and 20 percent of the technical schools managed by MOET are private.

The number of students who graduated from vocational training programs increased from 887,300 in 2001 to nearly 1.54 million in 2008. However, the large number of vocational training centers was still unable to supply sufficient numbers of skilled workers to meet the demands of industry in quality or quantity.

Institutional Weaknesses and Constraints

Several key institutional issues involving labor must be resolved before light manufacturing can reach its full potential in Vietnam.

Lack of Autonomy among Universities and Vocational Training Schools

The education system has not been able to facilitate the development of the skills required for an innovative workforce: the ability to solve real-world problems, to think critically, to work in teams, and to communicate effectively. Teaching methods (currently based on rote) and results assessments must be changed, and partnerships between universities and industry leaders must be fostered.

To enable universities and vocational schools to respond swiftly to the practical needs of the marketplace, more autonomy should be granted to such institutions. Currently, non-state universities need to obtain licenses every time a program is changed or developed. Vocational training schools have to follow the syllabi set by the GDVT and MOET.

Weak Links between Industry, Universities, and Vocational Schools

The majority of vocational training—about 60 percent of registered formal entities at various levels—is carried out by public and nonpublic TVET institutions that are not based on enterprises. The quality of the training in these institutions does not meet the demands of the labor market for many reasons. There is thus a weak link between industry and vocational schools and universities and a shortage of information on graduate employment, labor markets, and skills. These deficiencies are among the factors keeping education and skills training from responding to economic needs.

The lack of a connection with enterprises also results in limitations on the practical and pedagogical skills of vocational teachers and on the accessibility of trainees to modern equipment. MOLISA acknowledges that the cooperation between schools and businesses is tenuous and that vocational schools offer training courses based on their own resources and capacities, not on the demands of the business community.

Mismatch between the Training at Vocational Schools and the Needs of Industry

One of the most severe problems of the TVET system is the questionable quality and relevance of the training. Outdated and inflexible curricula that are not in tune with labor market demands are among the contributing factors. According to MOLISA regulations, vocational training schools must follow at least 70–80 percent of the training syllabi set by the ministries, giving schools little room to adjust to the changing needs of the labor market.[2]

Graduates of vocational training schools are not equipped with sufficient practical skills or knowledge about the work flow or workplace-specific behavior. For this reason, many employers must invest in skill upgrading before freshly hired TVET graduates can fulfill their tasks at work. The technology standards in vocational schools are also low. According to MOLISA, only 20 percent of all TVET institutions have modern equipment. The inadequate qualifications of TVET teachers, particularly the shortage of practical skills, aggravate the problem.

Surveys and other studies suggest there is a substantial degree of dissatisfaction among employers with the skills and competencies of the formally qualified workforce. The 2011 Provincial Competitiveness Index survey of the United States Agency for International Development and the Vietnam Chamber of Commerce and Industry revealed that, in a median province, 34.4 percent of the enterprises in the sample were dissatisfied with the availability and skill quality of labor (Malesky 2011). The survey also revealed that 47.4 percent of enterprises complained that they faced difficulty in recruiting skilled workers in 2009, up from 38.4 percent in 2008.

Despite the skilled labor shortages, a fairly large share of TVET graduates are unemployed. According to the 2009 Population and Housing Census conducted by the General Statistics Office, 81 percent of the 1.3 million unemployed have not had vocational training. However, 19 percent have had such training, highlighting the mismatch between the skills of TVET graduates and the needs of the labor market.

It is important that the responsible government agencies, such as the GDVT, encourage vocational schools to improve their programs by carefully analyzing industry needs. In addition, the government should urge high schools to cooperate with schools that provide vocational courses so that the high schools may promote vocational courses as an option. Industry requires more technicians, and not all high school graduates will be able to enroll in universities. To interest more high school students in vocational training programs, the transfer of vocational college graduates to university courses should be facilitated.

Unclear Division of Responsibilities between MOLISA and MOET

Two ministries are in charge of TVET. In 1998, the management of TVET was transferred from the Department of Technical and Vocational Education in MOET to the GDVT in MOLISA. MOET still manages higher technical education, and technical secondary education programs also remain the responsibility of MOET. The latter are at the lower secondary level, and their training content is similar to the vocational secondary programs administered by MOLISA. In addition, there is overlap between MOLISA and MOET college-level programs. This causes duplication in training and confusion among students.

According to the prevailing regulations, TVET institutions under MOET must follow the curricula set by the ministries and are subject to ministry supervision and certification. Similarly, TVET institutions under MOLISA must follow the curricula set by MOLISA. This has resulted in an unnecessary duplication or confusion in training curricula and the ineffective use of public funds for vocational and skill training.

An effective coordination mechanism for TVET departments within MOLISA and MOET does not exist. The unclear division of responsibilities between MOLISA and MOET represents an important management problem in the vocational training system and has been a negative factor in the effort to enhance worker skills. This ineffective coordination is one of the most important constraints on the TVET system (CIEM and NIVT 2012).

Labor Market Support Institutions Are Nascent

Other labor market institutions are still being established. The first employment service centers were launched in 1993. Currently, 130 employment centers have been set up, 64 of which are under the management of provincial MOLISA departments, while 66 are under the authority of various ministries, export management boards, or industrial zone management boards. However, these centers operate inefficiently because of a lack of funds, skills, and expertise, and their quality is uneven across the country.

Vietnam does not have an effective career guidance agency. Career advice and vocational navigation services aimed at young people are lacking, especially for high school graduates. Young graduates exhibit an overwhelming preference for universities over vocational schools. This represents an institutional constraint that needs to be addressed if the availability and quality of skilled workers are to be improved.

Public Institutions Are Underfunded, and Private Sector
TVET Investment Is Limited

Only public TVET institutions receive substantial public funding to cover capital and recurrent costs. However, actual allocations per student appear to be declining. For long-term programs administered by the GDVT, institutions receive public funding allocated through a per capita quota system. The budget norm per place is D 4.3 million a year (about $215), while actual allocations are often lower. Elementary TVET, which is provided in short courses, is not part of the quota system. Vocational training centers receive only a small amount of base funding from their parent sponsoring organizations. Underfunding therefore seems to be more severe in elementary TVET programs than at higher levels.

All public TVET institutions receive some subsidies for capital investment. To date, allocations per school are low and untargeted. In light of declining public per capita allocations, tuition fees have evolved into the most important source of income among TVET institutions. These fees are capped at D 120,000 a month at public institutions; so, most TVET institutions try to maximize enrollment to increase revenue. The current financing framework thus creates incentives to raise enrollment at the expense of the quality of training.

Private training providers have been growing in number in recent years. They are usually fully self-financing. Their main source of funding is tuition fees; they do not receive regular state funding. In line with its socialization policy, the government explicitly encourages the establishment of nonpublic training providers and has already set up a sound legal basis for the development of private institutions, including commercial schools. Nonetheless, the growth of the private TVET sector appears to be falling short of expectations because of ineffective implementation of support policies and the lack of competitiveness in private sector TVET. Except for state-owned enterprises (SOEs), companies show little incentive to invest in training.

Key Policy Recommendations: Labor Skills

The following policy measures should be taken to improve the availability and quality of skilled workers so that the country can move up the value added ladder:

- Strengthen the coordination between MOET and MOLISA. This is a critical step in the effort to enhance the TVET system.
- Ease the bureaucratic burden and administrative control of universities and TVET institutions and prioritize development so that university and TVET institution resources can be expended on meeting labor market demand and raising education standards.
- Orient vocational training toward the needs of business and industry. Systematic feedback from recent graduates about the workplace relevance of their courses and training programs should be collected to allow institutions to change curricula and programs. Graduate tracer studies will need to be carried out and used more effectively; the MOLISA labor force survey should

be improved and administered more regularly; and firm surveys or censuses should systematically collect information on skills from employers.

- Give universities and TVET institutions more autonomy, especially in adjusting curricula to labor market demands.
- Strengthen university-industry links and develop a regulatory framework that opens training and education providers up to dialogue with surrounding economic players, for example, through business, industry, and professional representation in education governing bodies, curriculum review committees, research review teams, and dissertation panels.
- Provide government incentives to develop a mechanism to encourage enterprises to receive student interns and create more incentives for work experience opportunities.
- Develop and implement an accreditation system among universities and TVET institutions.
- Encourage private investment in TVET by creating an explicit regulatory framework. This would include the privatization and equitization of public schools and new private investments, as well as increases in employer investments in TVET.
- Improve the financing of TVET institutions by issuing guidelines and regulations to govern the commercial income-generating activities of TVET institutions and by introducing financial TVET reforms that spread out training costs, including through more flexibility in increasing tuition fees.
- Strengthen the support for labor market institutions. Vocational navigation, career advice, and other services delivered by these labor market institutions should be enhanced.

Policy Recommendations in Light Manufacturing

Our main findings, including the key constraints and the policy actions needed to overcome them, are presented in annex table 9A.1. The table presents the measures required to bring about the much-needed structural transformation of the Vietnamese economy for significant and sustained growth in light manufacturing. The measures provide a reference point and define a medium- to long-term road map to full transformation to lift workers to higher productivity and more well-paying jobs.

The proposed measures cannot all be implemented at once; they need to be introduced sequentially in smaller packages. At any time, a limited number of the binding constraints—both cross-sectoral and sector specific—should be identified and addressed as a package over 12–18 months for maximum impact and with full institutional and financial support. The reform process should be continuous. As some measures become fully implemented, newer ones should be introduced to address the remaining binding constraints. The reform process should continue until the structural transformation is achieved. Note also that some of the proposed measures would benefit from additional discussions with stakeholders before they are adopted as concrete policy actions.

Factors of Success

Our detailed study (Dinh and others 2013) of how other countries harness light manufacturing to create jobs and prosperity highlights a number of success factors: creating a supportive environment for manufacturing, filling knowledge and financial gaps through foreign direct investment (FDI) and networks, starting small and building gradually, and establishing islands of success by keeping targeted policies selective and within a country's limited resources. In the context of Vietnam, the following policies are the most important.

Creating a Conducive Environment for Manufacturing

Policies in this area include public endorsement of growth and private sector development, flexible support by the government at each phase of the business life cycle, macroeconomic stability, appropriate trade policies, close public and private cooperation, and policies to enhance competition.

Public Endorsement of Economic Growth

Private manufacturing enterprises in Vietnam face an extremely high-risk environment that makes risk-adjusted rates of return appear low in the eyes of would-be entrepreneurs. Government commitment to industrial development, including strong public endorsement of economic growth and private sector development as a national priority, followed by action at both the local and national levels, helps reduce perceived risks.

Tailoring Government Support to the Business Life Cycle and Backing Winners

Our study shows that fruitful government support for manufacturing enterprises varies according to phases of the business life cycle. The support ranges from doing nothing to financing and facilitating enterprise growth, creating business incubators, and providing technology advisers. The government could advise firms on global market niches, cluster development, and business services such as customs and taxation. While government support is wide-ranging, including fiscal incentives, support for infrastructure development, and advisory support on upgrading, the assistance does not always involve heavy spending. Rather, the most effective form of government support is to identify, jointly with the private sector, the specific binding constraints in each sector and implement policies to remove these constraints. Identifying the most promising sectors does not involve picking winners, but backing winners, meaning that the government should follow the lead of the private sector in identifying industries and products to support, work closely with the private sector to find the most critical constraints affecting the growth of the industries and products that have been identified, and design policies to remove these constraints.

Macroeconomic Stability

Macroeconomic stability is an essential ingredient for successful development initiatives. In the successful cases that we have studied, entrepreneurs have benefited from policy stability, while in most of the unsuccessful cases, they have suffered from an unstable macroeconomic environment. In particular, maintaining a competitive exchange rate and avoiding inflation are especially important. In most of our case studies of failures, an overvalued or appreciating exchange rate hurt exports.

Trade Policies

The TPP, even more than previous trade agreements such as the World Trade Organization, will offer Vietnam an unprecedented opportunity to accelerate exports of manufacturing and therefore economic growth and job creation. At the same time, Vietnam has to be prepared to undertake reforms, especially reforms in SOEs, to benefit from the TPP. By and large, the TPP will help overcome the opposition of domestic vested interests to the structural reforms and will be crucial for industrialization in Vietnam.

Public-Private Cooperation

Close public and private cooperation is essential for any successful industrialization strategy. In many developing countries, the government eyes the private sector with suspicion, adopting a naive zero-sum perspective that considers private profit as a consequence of the exploitation or victimization of workers or customers and concludes that the state should capture and redistribute business profits. Such views encourage the private sector to regard government as a grabbing hand that aims to steal hard-won earnings from successful entrepreneurs. The case of China illustrates the potential for local governments to support and contribute actively to industrial development. China's experience in the development of clusters substantiates the argument that the government's role is to nurture and support existing cluster firms rather than trying to create clusters from scratch. Entrepreneurs rather than governments create clusters. Once clusters expand, the public sector can initiate a more active involvement to develop general infrastructure (roads, utilities, land) and target facilities to meet the specific requirements of emerging clusters (market structures, financial institutions, training programs, quality control mechanisms, and so on).

Competition

Competition is a key ingredient of the success of other East Asian countries. Chinese manufacturers report two sources of competition: fellow producers within the same province and producers outside the province. The central government in China has fostered nationwide competition by establishing awards and certifications that carry substantial monetary and reputational benefits. This is the positive role that competition plays in fostering group identification (Stiglitz 1992). Japan and the Republic of Korea have followed a similar path. China's local governments help firms develop competitive strength and pursue official awards and certifications, which can enlarge local budgets and enhance the reputation and career paths of local officials.

Filling Knowledge and Financial Gaps through FDI and Networks

The economic literature usually emphasizes the benefits of FDI in supplementing domestic savings. A lack of financial resources is only part of the problem, however. The lack of expertise, technology, and ideas is equally limiting, and both FDI and networks play a role in providing these elements of knowledge necessary for the development of enterprises and industries.

The East Asian countries that have successfully industrialized have relied on FDI to supply expertise, technology, and ideas through the associated foreign experts. China has followed this path. From the onset of the implementation of China's opening-up policy, which has lowered the barriers to international trade and private foreign investment, the Chinese economy has benefited from an influx of knowledge, capital, and market information. Chinese investors from Hong Kong SAR, China; Singapore; and Taiwan, China, whose linguistic and cultural affinity has facilitated easy communication, have been particularly influential. Bateman and Mody (1991), quoted in Romer (1993, 563), "observe that the best one-variable explanation for development in China, even if one restricts attention to the special economic zones, is geographic distance from Hong Kong SAR, China." The industrialization process in China has profited a great deal from the extensive network of Chinese living in Hong Kong SAR, China; in Macao SAR, China; and in Taiwan, China. For historical reasons, many Chinese who ran businesses in these locations were encouraged to come back, bringing with them not only capital, technology, and expertise, but also extensive social contacts and networks.

Education migrants have also contributed to the success of Chinese businesses; consider the many Chinese students enrolled in schools abroad. Precisely as in the case of Korea and of Taiwan, China, few of these students returned at first, leading to concerns about a loss of human capital. However, growing prosperity at home eventually induced many overseas graduates to come back. Even the graduates who remained abroad influenced the success of Chinese businesses through networks that created links between entrepreneurs abroad and researchers in China.

A similar immense advantage is available to Vietnam because of the large Vietnamese diaspora in Europe and North America that could be encouraged to return if the rules of the game were well defined.

FDI may compensate for deficiencies in education, managerial and entrepreneurial skills, technical expertise, commercial knowledge, and market information. In virtually all successful Chinese cases that we have studied, FDI has played a fundamental role not so much among domestic start-ups, but in the expansion of these firms when they require fresh technology, management expertise, marketing support, and finance. This has not been the case in the link between domestic producers in Vietnam and the large Vietnamese diaspora.

The tale of FDI is the same in other developing-country cases. The garment industry in Bangladesh illustrates clearly how FDI can combine with the domestic resources of a country to provide productive employment (Dinh and others 2013). What is striking in Bangladesh is the spillover: of 130 Bangladeshi sent to Korea for training, 115 had set up their own shops back in Bangladesh within seven years and had thus begun to contribute to the growth of their country's garment sector (Crook 1992). Over and over again, the role of FDI has been crucial.

The government could support the integration of supply chains in light manufacturing by encouraging FDI to take part in the upstream activities of the agribusiness, leather and shoe, wood, garment, and metal product sectors and by investing in industrial zones, especially plug-and-play zones, to help develop clusters in these sectors. Investment in marketplaces to facilitate market transactions would also be useful. This policy has been successfully adopted by various levels of government in China (Sonobe, Hu, and Otsuka 2002; Ding 2007; Ruan and Zhang 2009). The government of Vietnam could also provide financial incentives to increase investment in human managerial capital. For example, through adaptive research and training, the Industrial Technology Research Institute, in Taiwan, China, has facilitated imports of foreign technologies. The government of Vietnam could likewise invest in cluster-based infrastructure, such as roads and the supply of electricity. As firms expand production following successful quality improvements, they need more space and better infrastructure.

In the longer run, the government of Vietnam ought to consider encouraging strategic investment in selected companies abroad to gain advanced knowledge and technology in areas such as design and marketing in light manufacturing. Currently, outward investment flows are limited to oil companies, and the strategic advantages or strategic objectives of these flows are not clear.

Annex 9A: Policy Actions and Support Structures

Table 9A.1 A Complete Package of Policy Actions, Vietnam

Area	Short term	Medium term	Long term
Macrostability	Shift demand management policy from monetary to fiscal policy, which should aim at cutting the overall budget deficit by at least 3 percentage points per year, until the consolidated budget deficit is reduced to about 3 percent. Actively manage the capital account. Maintain flexibility in exchange rate policy, including readiness for sterilization; build up reserves. Use fiscal policy to contain inflation and move monetary policy toward management of capital flows and of long-run interest rates.	Develop financial markets. Redefine the role of the state to focus on a number of specific areas.	Same as medium term.
Industrial sector	From the highest level of government, issue forceful public endorsements of economic growth and private sector development as a key government priority.	Same as short term.	
	Undertake urgent reforms of the education and vocational systems, land, and input industries.	Same as short term.	
	Shift strategy from emphasis on creating new SMEs to making existing SMEs bigger through measures to address the dual industrial structure.	Same as short term.	Same as short term.

table continues next page

Table 9A.1 A Complete Package of Policy Actions, Vietnam (continued)

Area	Short term	Medium term	Long term
	Reform SOEs through the equitization of all enterprises in light manufacturing.	Continue the equitization and reform of SOEs in the other sectors.	Same as medium term.
	Provide equal treatment for direct and indirect exporters through (1) flexible and realistic exchange rates, (2) free trade in inputs and outputs, (3) competitive financial and money markets, (4) competitive primary input markets, and (5) nondiscriminatory domestic taxes. See chapter 3.	Same as short term.	
	Encourage the establishment and development of trading companies, first by focusing their activities on light manufacturing and in specific geographical areas.	Facilitate affordable housing in areas where businesses are concentrated, and set up industrial parks and sector clusters with residential facilities.	
	Encourage clusters through (a) investing in plug-and-play industrial zones and marketplaces to facilitate market transactions; (b) giving financial incentives to increase investment in managerial human capital; (c) investing in infrastructure, such as roads and electricity; as firms expand production following a successful quality improvement, they need more space and better infrastructure; (d) providing credit in the form of low-interest loans; the optimal credit policies would give credit only to firms that have established a record of successful innovation, and it would therefore be preferable to employ such policies during the quality improvement phase; and (e) offering fiscal incentives.	Same as short term.	Same as short term.
	Expand the social and foreign business network through policies to encourage the diaspora to come back and invest in light manufacturing.	Same as short term.	Encourage outward investment flows in selected companies abroad to gain knowledge and technology in design and marketing.
	Strengthen the subcontracting business by providing incentives to medium and large companies.	Same as short term.	Same as short term.
	Expand the Kaizen program to other areas.		
Apparel	Improve worker skills through training programs and technical assistance. See also measures on vocational training in chapter 9.	Same as short term.	Same as short term.
	Eliminate all import tariffs on apparel inputs, including those destined for small domestic producers.		
	Actively encourage cotton production and FDI in the spinning and weaving industries to supply capital, technology, and skill spillovers.	Same as short term.	Same as short term.
	Develop plug-and-play industrial parks in areas with potential to supply inputs.		

table continues next page

Table 9A.1 A Complete Package of Policy Actions, Vietnam (continued)

Area	Short term	Medium term	Long term
Leather and leather products	Improve worker skills through training programs and technical assistance. See also measures on vocational training in chapter 9.		
	Introduce local design and technical capabilities to develop local brands and product lines.		
	Encourage new investment in the tanning and leather products subsectors, which is absolutely essential for the renewal of the leather industry. This should be supplemented with training in entrepreneurship, management, and technical and design skills. Provide incentives to attract FDI to focus on the earlier stages of production, such as tanning, because these industries tend to be capital intensive and require highly skilled labor, which can only develop over time.	Same as short term.	Same as short term.
	Eliminate all import tariffs on leather inputs, and facilitate links between large exporters and small domestic producers.		
	Strengthen the role of subsectoral associations in the provision of advocacy and technical assistance.	Same a short term.	Commercialize the livestock subsector by encouraging ranch leasing and creating subsectoral clusters in appropriate locations.
	Enhance extension services, particularly in the areas of crossbreeding, disease control, slaughter training, preservation practices, quality improvement, and the potential value of hides and skins.	Same as short term.	Same as short term.
	Strengthen enforcement mechanisms to implement regulations related to the slaughtering, preservation, and transportation of livestock. Recruit, train, and employ independent inspectors and graders at collection centers.	Same as short term. Strengthen institutional capacity and policy coordination. Institutional capacity needs to be enhanced in both the public and private sectors.	Same as medium term.
Wood and wood products	Improve worker skills through formal and informal training (Kaizen) and through technical assistance. See also measures on vocational training in chapter 9.	Same as short term.	Improve incentives to encourage investment in plantation forestry.
	Encourage new investment and technology upgrades, including FDI, preferably in the form of joint ventures; training for technical and modern design skills; and new, integrated wood product clusters close to the source material.	Same as short term.	Same as short term.

table continues next page

Table 9A.1 A Complete Package of Policy Actions, Vietnam *(continued)*

Area	Short term	Medium term	Long term
	Develop plug-and-play industrial parks, which would help SMEs access utilities, land, finance, and skills through technical assistance programs for owner-managers and workers.		
	Encourage private sustainable plantations. Production plantations are still essential for maintaining sustainable forestry resources. It is necessary to stimulate private investment in plantation forestry to meet the future demand for fuelwood and also for the long-term supply for wood-based industries. Introduce more aggressive policy initiatives to comply with Forest Stewardship Council certification and rule of origin regulations.		
Metal products	Promote the exploitation of iron ore deposits, and conduct an in-depth feasibility study to assess the potential competitiveness of a domestic steel industry.		
	Develop plug-and-play industrial parks to facilitate access by SMEs to utilities, land, finance, and skills.		
	Promote foreign investment to make up for the capital shortage.		
Agribusiness	Facilitate commercial farming by establishing it in planned corridors. This initiative will require strong public-private partnerships to build the necessary infrastructure and arrange services, such as the leasing of farm machinery and equipment.	Set up agroprocessing clusters as part of special economic zones to encourage the processing industry.	Same as short term.
	Encourage contract farming to address the lack of access by small farmers to agricultural inputs and services and to formalize the connection between smallholders and the agroprocessing industry.	Same as short term.	Same as short term.
	Try a pilot approach for cluster formation.	Speed up cluster formation. Successful formation of clusters requires collaboration among the main stakeholders to build the necessary infrastructure, establish supply chain management, create training-with-production services, and develop market links.	Same as medium term.
	Enhance training services for food production under hygienic conditions. Scale up successful initiatives, such as the planned establishment of food processing training and production centers.	Same as short term.	Same as short term.
	Encourage the packaging industry by providing technical assistance to the agroprocessing sector. Conduct a feasibility study for investment in the production of packaging materials.		

Note: SME = small and medium enterprise; SOE = state-owned enterprise.

Light Manufacturing in Vietnam • http://dx.doi.org/10.1596/978-1-4648-0034-4

Figure 9A.1 The Cotton-to-Garment Market and Institutional Support Structure, China, 2010

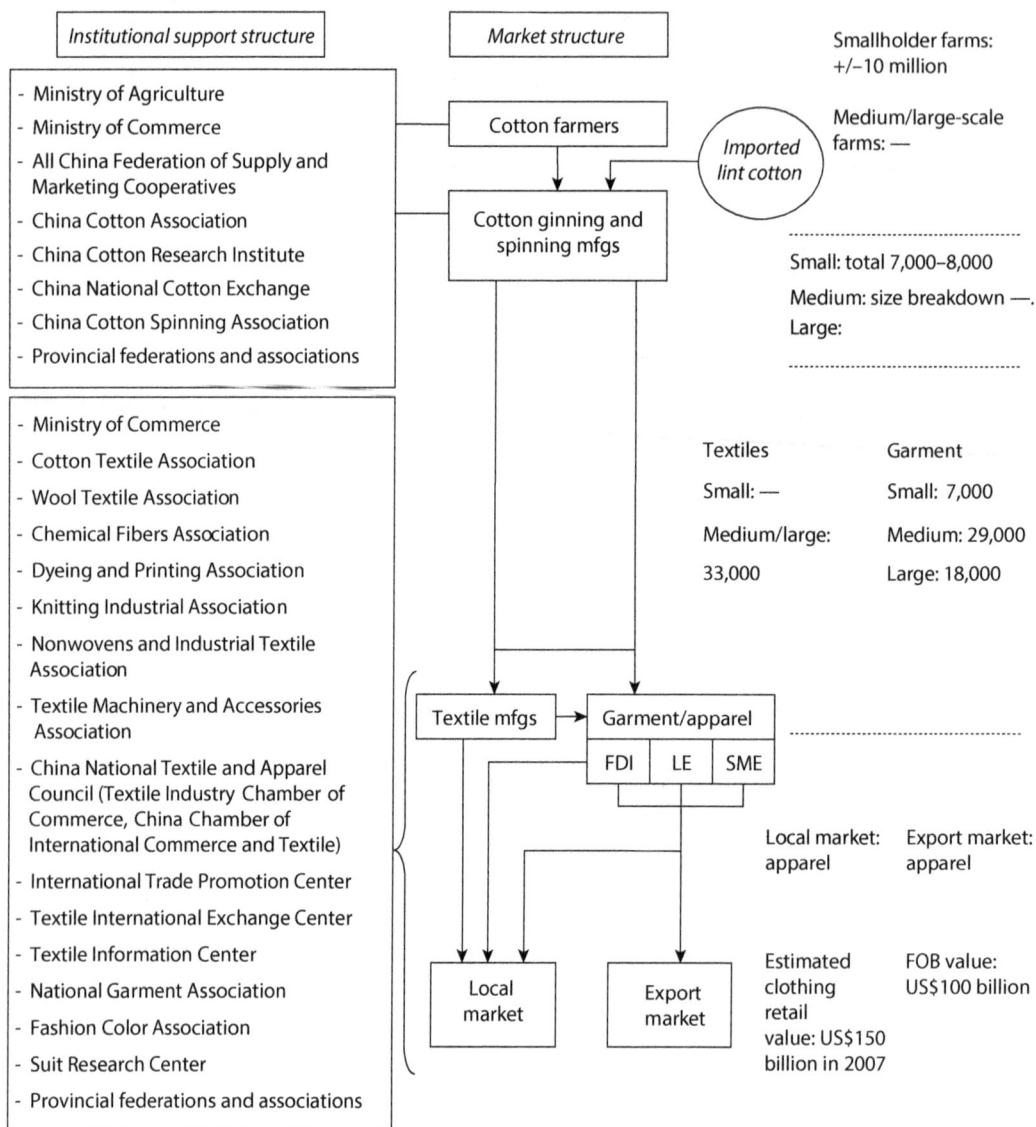

Institutional support structure	Market structure	
		Smallholder farms: +/–10 million

- Ministry of Agriculture
- Ministry of Commerce
- All China Federation of Supply and Marketing Cooperatives
- China Cotton Association
- China Cotton Research Institute
- China National Cotton Exchange
- China Cotton Spinning Association
- Provincial federations and associations

Cotton farmers

Imported lint cotton

Cotton ginning and spinning mfgs

Medium/large-scale farms: —

Small: total 7,000–8,000
Medium: size breakdown —.
Large:

- Ministry of Commerce
- Cotton Textile Association
- Wool Textile Association
- Chemical Fibers Association
- Dyeing and Printing Association
- Knitting Industrial Association
- Nonwovens and Industrial Textile Association
- Textile Machinery and Accessories Association
- China National Textile and Apparel Council (Textile Industry Chamber of Commerce, China Chamber of International Commerce and Textile)
- International Trade Promotion Center
- Textile International Exchange Center
- Textile Information Center
- National Garment Association
- Fashion Color Association
- Suit Research Center
- Provincial federations and associations

Textiles	Garment
Small: —	Small: 7,000
Medium/large:	Medium: 29,000
33,000	Large: 18,000

Textile mfgs

Garment/apparel
FDI | LE | SME

Local market: apparel

Export market: apparel

Local market

Export market

Estimated clothing retail value: US$150 billion in 2007

FOB value: US$100 billion

Source: GDS 2011.
Note: FDI = foreign direct investment enterprises; FOB = free on board production method; LE = large enterprises; mfgs = manufacturers; SME = small and medium enterprises; — = not available.

Figure 9A.2 The Cotton-to-Garment Market and Institutional Support Structure, Vietnam, 2010

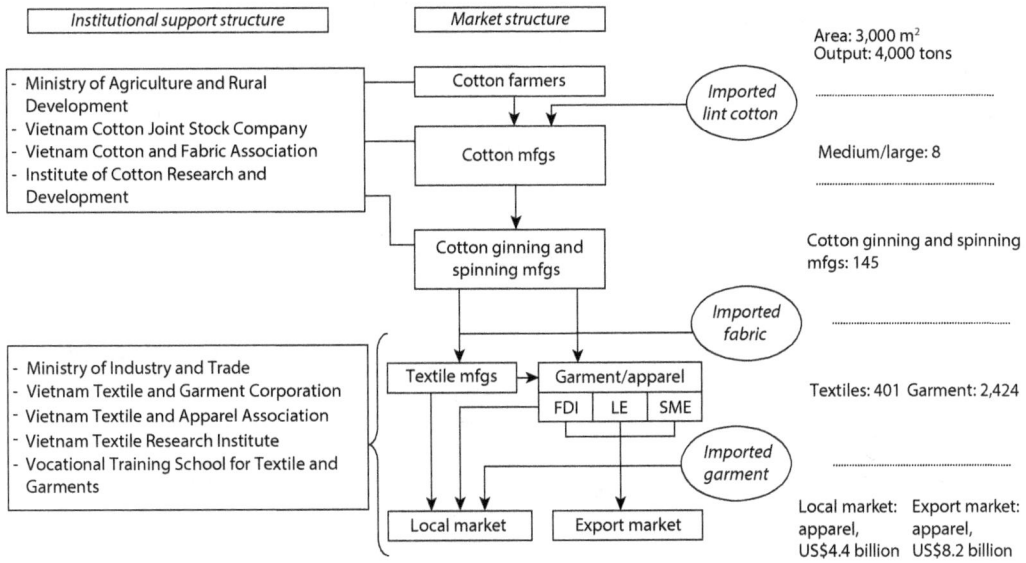

Source: GDS 2011.
Note: A dashed line indicates a weak link, a lack of organization, or areas where technical support is required to help strengthen links along the supply chain. FDI = foreign direct investment enterprises. LE = large enterprise; m² = square meter; mfgs = manufacturers; SME = small and medium enterprises.

Figure 9A.3 The Footwear Market and Institutional Support Structure, China, 2010

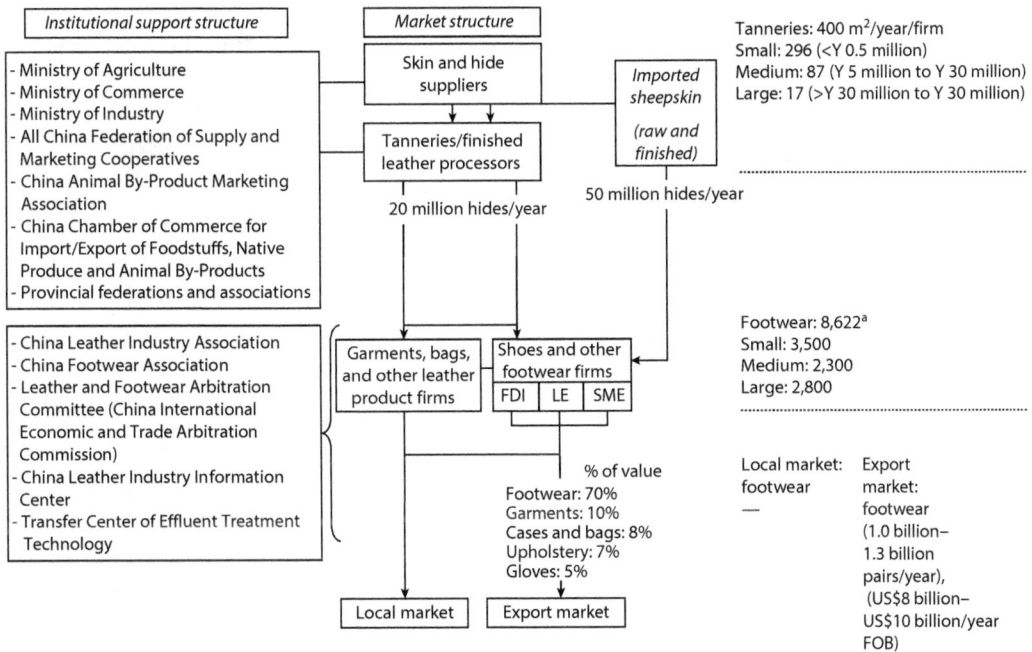

Source: GDS 2011.
Note: FDI = foreign direct investment enterprises; FOB = free on board production method; LE = large enterprise; m² = square meter; SME = small and medium enterprise; — = not available.
a. Fur and feather products included.

Figure 9A.4 The Footwear Market and Institutional Support Structure, Vietnam, 2010

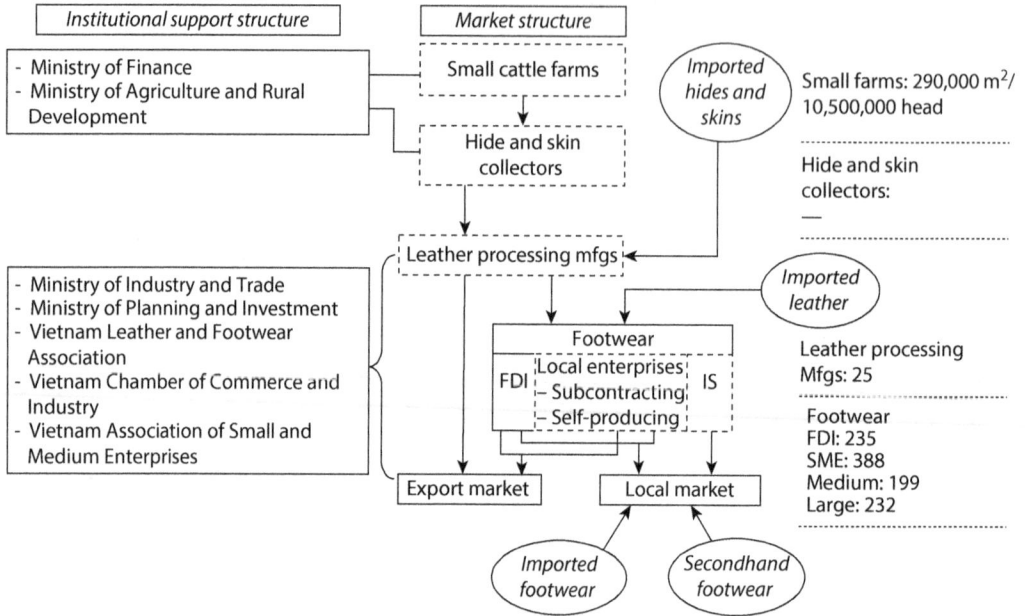

Institutional support structure	Market structure

- Ministry of Finance
- Ministry of Agriculture and Rural Development

Small cattle farms

Imported hides and skins

Small farms: 290,000 m²/ 10,500,000 head

Hide and skin collectors

Hide and skin collectors: —

- Ministry of Industry and Trade
- Ministry of Planning and Investment
- Vietnam Leather and Footwear Association
- Vietnam Chamber of Commerce and Industry
- Vietnam Association of Small and Medium Enterprises

Leather processing mfgs

Imported leather

Leather processing Mfgs: 25

Footwear
FDI Local enterprises IS
– Subcontracting
– Self-producing

Footwear
FDI: 235
SME: 388
Medium: 199
Large: 232

Export market   Local market

Imported footwear   Secondhand footwear

Source: GDS 2011.

Note: A dashed line indicates a weak link, a lack of organization, or areas where technical support is required to help strengthen links along the supply chain. FDI = foreign direct investment enterprises; IS = informal sector; mfgs = manufacturers; SME = small and medium enterprise; — = not available.

Figure 9A.5 The Wood Products Market and Institutional Support Structure, China, 2010

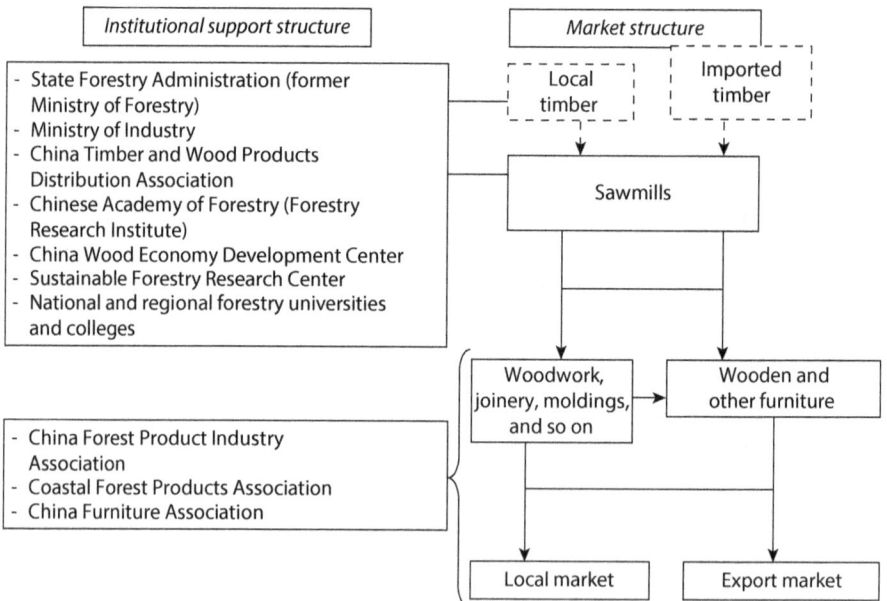

Institutional support structure	Market structure

- State Forestry Administration (former Ministry of Forestry)
- Ministry of Industry
- China Timber and Wood Products Distribution Association
- Chinese Academy of Forestry (Forestry Research Institute)
- China Wood Economy Development Center
- Sustainable Forestry Research Center
- National and regional forestry universities and colleges

Local timber   Imported timber

Sawmills

- China Forest Product Industry Association
- Coastal Forest Products Association
- China Furniture Association

Woodwork, joinery, moldings, and so on   Wooden and other furniture

Local market   Export market

Source: GDS 2011.

Note: A dashed line indicates a weak link, a lack of organization, or areas where technical support is required to help strengthen links along the supply chain.

Figure 9A.6 The Wood Products Market and Institutional Support Structure, Vietnam, 2010

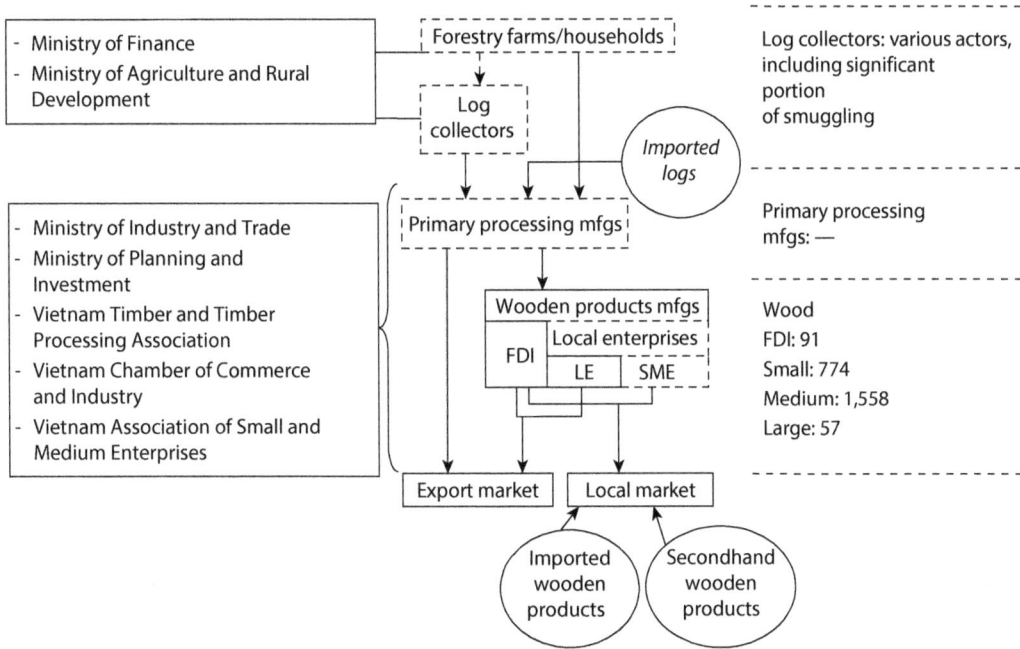

Source: GDS 2011.

Note: A dashed line indicates a weak link, a lack of organization, or areas where technical support is required to help strengthen links along the supply chain. FDI = foreign direct investment enterprises; LE = large enterprise; mfgs = manufacturers; SME = small and medium enterprise.

Figure 9A.7 The Wood Processing Road Map, Vietnam, 2010

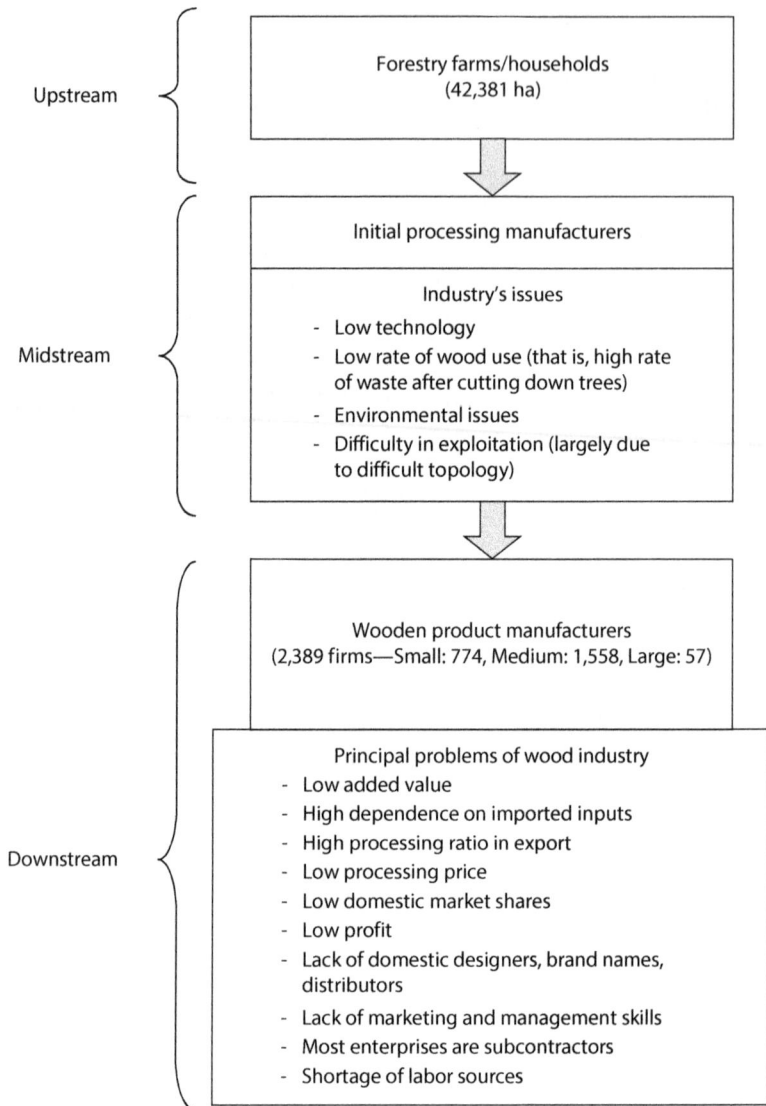

Upstream
> **Forestry farms/households**
> (42,381 ha)

Midstream
> **Initial processing manufacturers**
>
> Industry's issues
> - Low technology
> - Low rate of wood use (that is, high rate of waste after cutting down trees)
> - Environmental issues
> - Difficulty in exploitation (largely due to difficult topology)

Downstream
> **Wooden product manufacturers**
> (2,389 firms—Small: 774, Medium: 1,558, Large: 57)
>
> Principal problems of wood industry
> - Low added value
> - High dependence on imported inputs
> - High processing ratio in export
> - Low processing price
> - Low domestic market shares
> - Low profit
> - Lack of domestic designers, brand names, distributors
> - Lack of marketing and management skills
> - Most enterprises are subcontractors
> - Shortage of labor sources

Source: GDS 2011.
Note: ha = hectare.

Figure 9A.8 The Metal Products Market and Institutional Support Structure, China, 2010

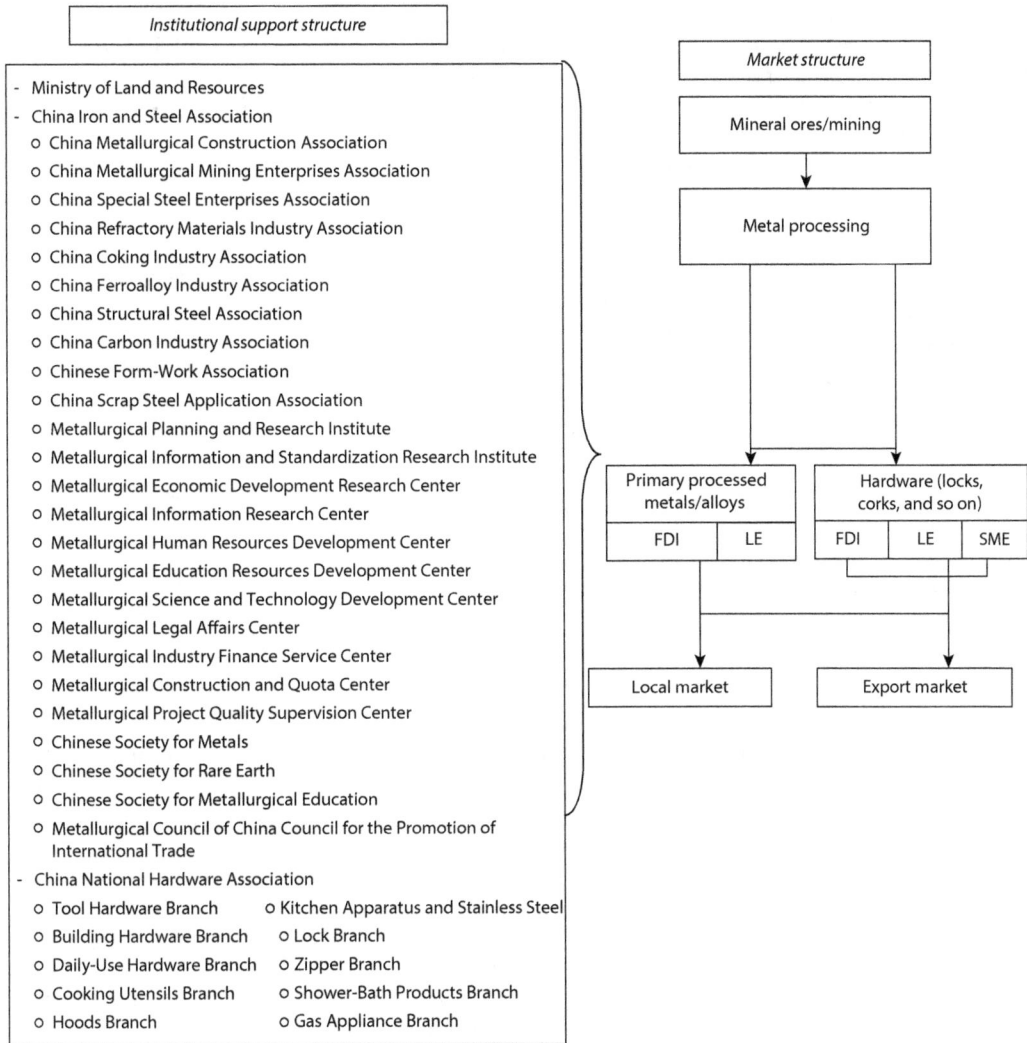

Institutional support structure

- Ministry of Land and Resources
- China Iron and Steel Association
  - China Metallurgical Construction Association
  - China Metallurgical Mining Enterprises Association
  - China Special Steel Enterprises Association
  - China Refractory Materials Industry Association
  - China Coking Industry Association
  - China Ferroalloy Industry Association
  - China Structural Steel Association
  - China Carbon Industry Association
  - Chinese Form-Work Association
  - China Scrap Steel Application Association
  - Metallurgical Planning and Research Institute
  - Metallurgical Information and Standardization Research Institute
  - Metallurgical Economic Development Research Center
  - Metallurgical Information Research Center
  - Metallurgical Human Resources Development Center
  - Metallurgical Education Resources Development Center
  - Metallurgical Science and Technology Development Center
  - Metallurgical Legal Affairs Center
  - Metallurgical Industry Finance Service Center
  - Metallurgical Construction and Quota Center
  - Metallurgical Project Quality Supervision Center
  - Chinese Society for Metals
  - Chinese Society for Rare Earth
  - Chinese Society for Metallurgical Education
  - Metallurgical Council of China Council for the Promotion of International Trade
- China National Hardware Association
  - Tool Hardware Branch
  - Building Hardware Branch
  - Daily-Use Hardware Branch
  - Cooking Utensils Branch
  - Hoods Branch
  - Kitchen Apparatus and Stainless Steel
  - Lock Branch
  - Zipper Branch
  - Shower-Bath Products Branch
  - Gas Appliance Branch

Market structure

Mineral ores/mining → Metal processing → Primary processed metals/alloys (FDI | LE) / Hardware (locks, corks, and so on) (FDI | LE | SME) → Local market / Export market

Source: GDS 2011.
Note: FDI = foreign direct investment enterprises; LE = large enterprise; SME = small and medium enterprise.

Figure 9A.9 The Iron Ore-to-Steel Market and Institutional Support Structure, Vietnam, 2010

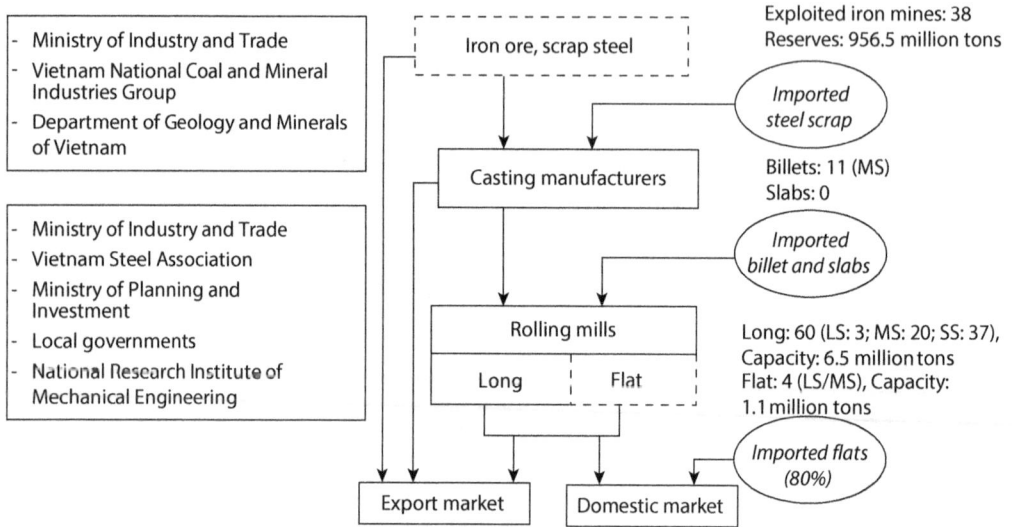

Source: GDS 2011.

Note: A dashed line indicates a weak link, a lack of organization, or areas where technical support is required to help strengthen links along the supply chain. LS = large scale; MS = medium scale; SS = small scale.

Notes

1. This section on institutional constraints on labor skills has been prepared by Pham Ngoc Thach.

2. Decision 58/2008/QĐ-BLDTBXH of June 9, 2008, Ministry of Labor, Invalids, and Social Affairs, Hanoi.

References

Bateman, Deborah A., and Askoka Mody. 1991. "Growth in an Inefficient Economy: A Chinese Case Study." World Bank, Washington, DC.

Chenery, Hollis B. 1979. *Structural Change and Development Policy.* Oxford, U.K.: Oxford University Press.

CIEM (Central Institute for Economic Management) and NIVT (National Institute for Vocational Training). 2012. "Improving the Relevance of the TVET System to the Needs of the Business Sector: Final Report." CIEM and NIVT, Hanoi. http://www .markets4poor.org/m4p2/filedownload/Final_report_CIEM_NIVT_EN%20(final%20 revision).pdf.

Crook, Clive. 1992. "Third World Economic Development." Online Library of Economics and Liberty. http://www.econlib.org/library/Enc1/ThirdWorldEconomicDevelopment .html.

Ding, Ke. 2007. "Domestic Market-Based Industrial Cluster Development in Modern China." IDE Discussion Paper 88, Institute of Developing Economies, Japan External Trade Organization, Tokyo.

Dinh, Hinh T., Vincent Palmade, Vandana Chandra, and Frances Cossar. 2012. *Light Manufacturing in Africa: Targeted Policies to Enhance Private Investment and Create Jobs.* Washington, DC: World Bank. http://go.worldbank.org/ASG0J44350.

Dinh, Hinh T., Thomas G. Rawski, Ali Zafar, Lihong Wang, and Eleonora Mavroeidi. 2013. *Tales from the Development Frontier: How China and Other Countries Harness Light Manufacturing to Create Jobs and Prosperity.* With Xin Tong and Pengfei Li. Washington, DC: World Bank.

GDS (Global Development Solutions). 2011. *The Value Chain and Feasibility Analysis; Domestic Resource Cost Analysis.* Vol. 2 of *Light Manufacturing in Africa: Targeted Policies to Enhance Private Investment and Create Jobs.* Washington, DC: World Bank. http://go.worldbank.org/6G2A3TFI20.

Hausmann, Ricardo, Dani Rodrik, and Andrés Velasco. 2005. "Growth Diagnostics." John F. Kennedy School of Government, Harvard University, Cambridge, MA.

Malesky, Edmund. 2011. "The Vietnam Provincial Competitiveness Index 2011: Measuring Economic Governance for Business Development." USAID-VNCI Policy Paper 16, Vietnam Competitiveness Initiative (Vietnam Chamber of Commerce and Industry and United States Agency for International Development), Hanoi. http://vietnam .usaid.gov/sites/default/files/usaid_vnci_no16_pci_2011_final_web_0.pdf.

MOLISA (Ministry of Labor, Invalids, and Social Affairs). 2011. "Vietnam Employment Trends 2010." Office of the International Labour Organization in Vietnam and National Center for Labor Market Forecast and Information, Bureau of Employment, MOLISA, Hanoi. http://www.ilo.org/wcmsp5/groups/public/—asia/—ro-bangkok /—ilo-hanoi/documents/publication/wcms_151318.pdf.

Mori, Junichi, Pham T. Hoang, and Nguyen T. X. Thuy. 2010. "Survey Report: Quality of Technical and Vocational Education and Training: Perceptions of Enterprises in Hanoi and Surrounding Provinces." Vietnam Development Forum, National Graduate Institute for Policy Studies, Tokyo. http://www.grips.ac.jp/vietnam/VDFTokyo /download.html.

Romer, Paul. 1993. "Idea Gaps and Object Gaps in Economic Development." *Journal of Monetary Economics* 32 (3): 543–73.

Ruan, Jianqing, and Xiaobo Zhang. 2009. "Finance and Cluster-Based Industrial Development in China." *Economic Development and Cultural Change* 58 (1): 143–64.

Sonobe, Tetsushi, Dinghuan Hu, and Keijiro Otsuka. 2002. "Process of Cluster Formation in China: A Case Study of a Garment Town." *Journal of Development Studies* 39 (1): 118–39.

Stiglitz, Joseph E. 1992. "The Meanings of Competition in Economic Analysis." *Rivista Internazionale di Scienze Sociali* 100 (2): 191–212.

The Methodology of the Comparative Value Chain Analysis

The analyses in chapters 4–8 reflect the work of our consultant firm, Global Development Solutions, LLC., based on the benchmarking of productivity and costs among mostly formal medium firms in China and Vietnam (see GDS 2011). To ensure the comparability of performance benchmarks, we have chosen important representative products for the value chain and feasibility analyses: polo shirts and men's underwear for apparel, leather shoes and golf gloves for leather products, wooden chairs and doors for wood products, crown corks and padlocks for metal products, milling for wheat products, and milk for dairy products. We also selected these products based on the fact that they are being produced through simple, labor-intensive manufacturing processes that are similar across all comparator countries. The technical specifications for each product are shown in table A.1.

The analyses are based on in-depth interviews (including data collection on cost and productivity) at more than 300 formal medium firms producing these products in the five countries in our study: China, Ethiopia, Tanzania, Vietnam, and Zambia (see table A.2 for the numbers in China and Vietnam). Data were collected between July 2010 and February 2011.

The drivers of firm competitiveness (productivity and cost) have been systematically decomposed and benchmarked according to the following framework:

- Labor cost (wages) differentiated by skilled and unskilled labor
- Labor efficiency (pieces per worker per day, product reject rates)
- Capital cost (machines, buildings, and land)
- Capital efficiency (capacity use)
- Input cost (adjusted for quality)
- Input efficiency (material waste)
- Utility cost and usage
- Financing cost
- Logistics cost
- Overhead and other regulatory cost (for example, taxes)
- Quality (quality of product and delivery; brand and firm reputation)

Table A.1 Technical Specifications of the Products under Study

| Product | Weight | | Dimension | | | | |
	Weight	Unit of measure	As indicated			Unit of measure	Material
1 Golf glove	85–141	Grams				Men's medium	Sheepskin
2 Loafer	780	Grams	Heel	Width	Insole	Centimeters	Sheepskin
Size	United States, 8	European Union, 7	2.5	10	30	n.a.	n.a.
3 Padlock[a]	760	Grams	7	7	—[a]	Centimeters	Brass
4 Crown cork (bottle cap)[b]	290	Milligrams	Thickness 0.24	Diameter 31.9	Height 6.6	Millimeters	Tin-free steel
5 Wooden chair	6.5	Kilograms	Width 45	Depth 45	Height 75	Centimeters	Pine
6 Wooden door	12	Kilograms	Width 80	Depth 4	Height 210	Centimeters	Pine
7 Milk	0.5	Liters	Protein 3.5%	Lactose 4.7%	Ash 0.8%	Vitamins B1, B2, C, and D	Fat content Full
8 Milling	Type, German	Type, French	Ash	Protein	Moisture	All-purpose flour	Wheat or rice
	550	55	<0.65%	≈11%	<14.5%		
9 Polo shirt	250–270	Grams	n.a.	n.a.	n.a.	n.a.	100% cotton

Source: GDS 2011.
Note: — = not available; n.a. = not applicable.
a. According to the photo provided by the study team, overall height is 14 centimeters, and the shackle has a diameter of 2 centimeters.
b. The weight of the cover—a plastic sole made of polyvinyl chloride—in the internal surface of the cap is 290 milligrams.

Table A.2 Interviews Conducted for the Value Chain Study, China and Vietnam

Sector	China	Vietnam
Apparel	16	8
Leather	14	12
Wood	16	12
Metal	12	10
Agribusiness	20	18
Total	78	60

Source: GDS 2011.

The total costs have been allocated pro rata to the products under study in the overall production of the firms. Because the focus is on simple labor-intensive light manufacturing products, most of the costs are variable (for example, inputs, direct labor, and logistics).

Our examination of the reasons for the main differences in productivity and cost provides insights on the main external constraints (for example, government policies) affecting the competitiveness of firms in each sector. This methodology has the following limitations (and, for this reason, needs to be complemented with the other instruments discussed in the chapters):

- It focuses mostly on formal medium firms, excluding the huge segment of small informal firms.
- It relies on fairly small samples of firms.
- It relies on observations of the productivity and costs of existing firms that may have had better access to key inputs and factors of production. We try to analyze how differentiated access is affected by the policy environments in each country for different types of players. In addition, we have analyzed the conditions of access for small firms.

Reference

GDS (Global Development Solutions). 2011. *The Value Chain and Feasibility Analysis; Domestic Resource Cost Analysis.* Vol. 2 of *Light Manufacturing in Africa: Targeted Policies to Enhance Private Investment and Create Jobs.* Washington, DC: World Bank. http://go.worldbank.org/6G2A3TFI20.

Environmental Benefits Statement

The World Bank Group is committed to reducing its environmental footprint. In support of this commitment, the Publishing and Knowledge Division leverages electronic publishing options and print-on-demand technology, which is located in regional hubs worldwide. Together, these initiatives enable print runs to be lowered and shipping distances decreased, resulting in reduced paper consumption, chemical use, greenhouse gas emissions, and waste.

The Publishing and Knowledge Division follows the recommended standards for paper use set by the Green Press Initiative. Whenever possible, books are printed on 50 percent to 100 percent postconsumer recycled paper, and at least 50 percent of the fiber in our book paper is either unbleached or bleached using Totally Chlorine Free (TCF), Processed Chlorine Free (PCF), or Enhanced Elemental Chlorine Free (EECF) processes.

More information about the Bank's environmental philosophy can be found at http://crinfo.worldbank.org/wbcrinfo/node/4.

green press
INITIATIVE